CW00621859

simple

simple

Justice, wealth and eco-Christianity Helen Jaeger

© Helen Jaeger 2003

ISBN 1 85999 641 8

SUbtle products are youth publications of
Scripture Union, 207-209 Queensway, Bletchley, MK2 2EB, England
Email: info@scriptureunion.org.uk
Website: www.scriptureunion.org.uk

Scripture Union Australia
Locked Bag 2, Central Coast Business Centre, NSW 2252, Australia
Website: www.su.org.au

Scripture Union USA
P.O. Box 987, Valley Forge, PA 19482
www.scriptureunion.org

All rights reserved. No part of this publication may be reproduced, stored in a
retrieval system, or transmitted, in any form or by any means, electronic,
mechanical, photocopying, recording or otherwise, without the prior permission
of Scripture Union.

The right of Helen Jaeger to be identified as author of this work has been asserted
by her in accordance with the Copyright, Designs and Patents Act 1988.

Scripture quotations taken from the HOLY BIBLE NEW INTERNATIONAL
INCLUSIVE LANGUAGE VERSION © 1973, 1978, 1984 by International Bible Society.
Anglicisation copyright © 1979, 1984, 1989. Used by
permission of Hodder & Stoughton Ltd.

British Library Cataloguing-in-Publication Data
A catalogue record for this book is available from the British Library.

Cover design by Martin Lore
Printed and bound in Great Britain by Creative Print and Design (Wales) Ebbw Vale

Scripture Union is an international Christian charity working with churches in
more than 130 countries providing resources to bring the good news about Jesus
Christ to children, young people and families – and to encourage them to develop
spiritually through the Bible and prayer. As well as our network of volunteers, staff
and associates who run holidays, church-based events and school Christian groups,
we produce a wide range of publications and support those who use our resources
through training programmes.

For Andy,
chocolate-provider and encourager

Contents

SECTION ONE:

JUSTICE

Chapter one

Guilty as charged

I have to confess that I was brought up as a Catholic and yes, the greetings card that has some hapless soul writing on a blackboard in front of a nun the lines 'I am personally responsible for the suffering of Christ' does make me laugh. Yes, there was church every single Sunday until I was 18, as well as high days and holy days (sort of religious bank holidays, but where you have to go to church). Yes, there was confession in a small, musty, wooden confessional box speaking through a grille to a bloke who would later be coming round for a Sunday roast dinner. Yes, the nuns wore so much polyester you thought they'd be whipped off to heaven any second in a fatal flash of static. Yes, there were fish-only Fridays (though my family managed to stretch it to takeaway fish 'n' chips – a cunning reinterpretation that turned what should have been a day of semi-fasting in remembrance of Jesus' death into something we could actually all look forward to). And yes, there was communion (white dress, veils and shoes and a new shiny red Bible), Catholic school (class mass with readings and a few well-chosen hymns on the plastic piano) and nun night-class discussing the finer points of faith on a Thursday evening.

But also – and this is where I have to come really clean – there was wonder about creation, there was an appreciation of the world, not a shying away from it, and there were moments of genuinely meeting God. Like the unexplained light-hearted feeling you'd get after you'd confessed for the millionth time to nicking your brother's pocket money and kicking the cat. Like sitting in the Church of Reconciliation in that Catholic hot spot, Walsingham, and feeling the deepest, sunniest sense of peace you'd ever felt. Like praying to your Sacred Heart Jesus statue about your exams and the weather for Wednesday's netball match and whatever else you felt like praying about. And there was just simply being able to believe.

Finally there was the fact that the Catholic church, for all its faults and failings, has a long list of people it calls saints, who cared for the poor, healed the sick, fought for social justice and celebrated creation. In fact, it's taken for granted not only that you will want to know about these role models of the faith, but also that you will want to copy the best characteristics of the ones that appeal to you. Aged 11, you are faced with the choice of who to choose as your confirmation saint – mine was Francis, because my saints' book had a picture of him grinning broadly and preaching to a line of birds perched on his outstretched arms. Also, he gave up all his money and privilege to serve the poor, which appealed to the tender rebel in me.

Happy, clappy, dippy?

So it was with some amazement that I rolled up a few years later at a charismatic new church, straight out of college, renewed in my beliefs, fresh out of an encounter with the Holy Spirit (that happened in a church where people were dancing with ribbons, but let's not go there) and ready and raring to change the world, to find that you could do it only if you were a) a preacher or b) a worship leader. At least, that was the impression you got if you read the recommended books, listened to the talks and even heard the prophecies. So who were the role models in this particular neck of the woods? Certainly not the defiant activists like Oscar Romero, the guerrilla-warfare-defying nuns in Nicaragua or the Mother Teresas I'd grown up with.

There were the men who had died trying to convert the obscure South American tribes (preachers). The men who had started revival here and in America (preachers). And that was about it. Women who cared about social justice were relegated to Greenham Common and their spirituality was viewed as suspect. I think men who cared about social justice and the poor probably felt the same way, too – once they grew up they'd want to be preachers and worship leaders too. And the prophecies – did I ever hear one about good news to the poor? Maybe twice. There was a lot more about revival, about the lost (but not necessarily the poor lost) and, you guessed it, preaching.

Feed your heart and head

I think we are doing ourselves a disservice by being so narrow, which is why this little book is in your hands. You want justice. You're drawn to it. You see it's real and necessary. But maybe no one seems to be talking about it that much. Well, welcome: come in and sit yourself down. If you hunger and thirst for it, this book may be at least a snack that keeps you going as you search out the big meal – bringing about the real thing in the wonderful, messy, messed-up world of which we're privileged to be a part.

> 'Blessed are those who hunger and thirst for righteousness, for they will be filled.'
> (Matthew 5:6)

Chapter two

Justice – just a nice idea?

You may have wondered whether this justice thing really is a big deal or whether it's just an excuse for people with attitude to thump the table and shout a lot. Well, first up, let's take a quick tour through the Bible.

A few chapters into the good book, God is kicking our great-great-great-to-the-power-100 grandparents out of their rural idyll because they did the one thing he asked them not to. Fair? Sure was. He had, after all, warned them. Next chapter, Cain is cutting up his brother in a fit of my-sacrifice-is-better-than-yours jealousy. God finds out and banishes the murderous sibling to a city of refuge (justice mixed with mercy – a potent combination). Then there's the giving of the law in Exodus, which is chock-a-block with just laws (eg Exodus 23). Next we move into prophets confronting bad kings and queens (1 Kings), a major section about what Jesus will be like in Isaiah 42 (justice-establisher is one of his characteristics) and a whole raft of minor prophets insulting the heartless wealthy of their day and challenging Israel, because it cares more about singing and services than justice for the poor and a right relationship with God. But is justice simply an angry Old Testament kind of a thing?

Certainly not. Moving on to the New Testament, Jesus puts justice and concern for the poor right at the heart of his ministry and vision. It's a theme continued by Jesus' close disciples. For example, James gives those who favour the rich a hearty wrist-slapping as they attempt to jostle Mr and Mrs Considerably-Richer-Than-You in front of their poorer church friends at the annual summer picnic (James 2). Even at the big, scary, trembling-knees judgement moment, Jesus warns us (lovingly) that we will be judged more on whether we fed the hungry, clothed the naked, visited the sick – in short, had a heart for social justice and the poor – than on whether we sang 'I wanna see Jesus lifted high' with the correct arm actions.

> **But if your image of justice is funny wigs, court-rooms and fat lawyer salaries, reflect on this: justice in the Bible is 100 per cent Value-Brand, everyday-lifeness. It's to do with you, me and how we get on.**

Let's go deeper...

In the Old Testament, ordinary people sought justice. Crime is a major relationship-wrecker, so justice is about getting the victim, the wrongdoer and their community sorted. It's not just kiss-and-make-up. Justice as God set it out was practical, problem-solving and forward-thinking. Things don't change by the time we get to the New Testament. Check out Zacchaeus (Luke 19:10), who, after Jesus has told everyone 'Party. Zacchaeus' place – now', decides to pay people back four times over the amount he's ripped them off. His neighbours accept him back and a wrong is righted. This is justice and it's real, not limited to philosophy or unreadable books.

Justice: rough guide

Places to stay: real key bits of the Bible to keep coming back to

- Justice is about freedom. (Psalm 103)
- God's into justice and wants us to be, too. (Isaiah 58, Matthew 12)
- God's particularly concerned about people who might be denied justice – the poor 'n' powerless. (Psalm 140:12)

> *Places to eat: get fed, tasty stuff*
>
> - God honours our justice-choosing attitudes (1 Kings 3:11).
> - As a Christian, you too can do it (Hebrews 11:32–34).
> - Jesus was denied justice (Acts 8:33), so even when we experience injustice ourselves, God completely understands and has been there before us.
> - God does not withhold justice (Luke 18).

Have a little fun

Maybe you reckon justice is a load of bad hair days piled together. Sometimes the way people do justice, it can seem both worthy and dull! No wonder we want to steer clear. But in fact, the Bible makes it clear there's a DIRECT link between joy and justice (Proverbs 21:15), so party and protest really do go hand in hand. Injustice, not justice, is the real killjoy.

In fact, here are some of the weirder things people have got up to in the name of demanding justice. Freak or unique? You decide. Sailing round whales; scaling Big Ben; putting a flower in a soldier's rifle; throwing free raves; setting up long-term protest camps; standing defenceless in front of a tank; living in trees; exposing destructive mining; turfing roads; distributing alternative news; being chained to the London Eye; living underground; squatting; refusing to pay tax; warehouse partying; kidnapping MPs; trashing fighter planes; throwing away all supermarket packaging in-shop; going to prison; infiltrating bad businesses; confronting sleazy double-dealing politicians.

Put like that, justice sounds radical, exciting, desirable, necessary and a load of other things that get me leaping around thinking 'yes, I'm a believer! And God is into this stuff, too!!*'. And if you still don't believe that the Bible, God or godly people have anything to say about justice, check out the following chapter.

(*OK, maybe not all the illegal bits.)

Chapter three

CAUTION: JUST GOD AT WORK

Genesis 49:15–17
Exodus 23:1–7
Deuteronomy 18–21
Deuteronomy 27:18–20
1 Kings 10:8–10
2 Chronicles 9:7–9
2 Chronicles 19:5–8
Job 5:15,16
Job 29:13–16
Job 31:12–14
Job 34:16–19
Job 36:2–4
Job 36:16–18
Job 37:22–24
Psalm 36:5–7
Psalm 37:27,28
Psalm 45:5–7
Psalm 64:5–7
Psalm 89:13–15
Psalm 97:1–3
Psalm 103:5–7
Psalm 140:11–13
Proverbs 13:22–23
Proverbs 21:14–16
Proverbs 29:3–8
Ecclesiastes 5:8–9
Isaiah 5:22–24
Isaiah 9:6–8
Isaiah 10:1–3
Isaiah 11:3–5

Isaiah 16:4–6
Isaiah 28:5–7
Isaiah 28:16–18
Isaiah 32:15–17
Isaiah 33:4–6
Isaiah 42:1–2
Isaiah 42:3–5
Isaiah 51:3–6
Isaiah 56:1–2
Isaiah 58:5–7
Isaiah 59:7–10
Isaiah 59:13–15
Jeremiah 9:23,24
Jeremiah 21:11–14
Amos 2:6–8
Amos 5:11–13
Amos 5:14–16
Amos 5:23–25
Amos 6:11–13
Micah 3:7–10
Habakkuk 1:3–5
Matthew 12:17–19
Matthew 12:19–21
Luke 18:2–5
Luke 18:6–8
Acts 17:30–32
Romans 3:25–27
2 Corinthians 7:10–12
Revelation 19:10–12

Check out any of the above and you'll find something about justice. As a word, it's mentioned in over half the books of the Bible, but even where it's not called by name, you'd have to be reading a different book not to think God cares about it. Like a stick of rock, cut God and you'll find that one of the words that runs straight through him for all time is Justice. Like a hallmark that distinguishes a bit of silver from silver-sprayed tat, every action of God's passes the 'yes, it's just' test and gets stamped as authentic.

And it's just the kind of stuff he's still up to in the twenty-first century.

God in the world

God is at work with global acts of awesome dexterity (the Berlin Wall toppling, the Good Friday Agreement, the end of apartheid in South Africa, the election of one formerly oppressed, Nelson Mandela). And it's not just nations and power brokers God's concerned about. Justice is breaking out all over the place, if only we have eyes to see it.

God in her life

Take this story about a friend of mine. My friend was working as a teacher and enjoying her work. Then her head of department, with whom she was really good friends, left. To start with, the pressure was kept minimal – just a few hours after school here and a bit of pressure to take on extra work there. Then it cranked up a gear – my friend was put in charge of teaching subjects of which she had no experience. She felt bad about this, as it meant that the students weren't getting a fair deal. When she raised the issue, she was told that no one else could do it, even though she was a new teacher and should have been having time off to be supported.

Then there was the day a group of her colleagues decided she was next in line for a bit of whispering and gossiping, not least because she'd started a prayer group at the school. Finally, another guy was appointed to teach. This guy was vehemently anti-Christian and took every opportunity to disparage her work (including in front of the classes she taught) and before her colleagues. He made fun of her faith and generally made her life less than something to wake up to on a Monday morning thinking, 'Hey, fab.' About the same time, her head teacher told her he would give her the qualification she was working for early, if she gave up her job, because he could get someone cheaper to do it. When he discovered he couldn't, he took back his offer and it was back to the overwork number. Finally, my friend injured herself physically and was signed off sick. You know what her colleagues decided to think? That this was just a massive plan to skive. The head teacher wrote to her doctor alleging she wasn't ill at all and actually needed psychiatric help!

This tale of woe and injustice looked as if it could run and run, but luckily my friend's doctor took one look at the letter, declared it spiteful and untrue, and told her he would sign her off for as long as she needed him to.

But it didn't end there. A God of justice isn't satisfied with half-measures. My friend had been offered a job at another school. She'd accepted it, even though her Christian-persecuting colleague had told her the school would take her only because she was cheap (being less experienced). However, there were problems with her contract. It looked as if she wouldn't be able to take the new job. Then her new head teacher rang her and told her he would be sorting out the contract – he was legally bound to honour the offer of a job. He offered to do all the negotiations himself (her old school were trying both to slag her off and to get her back at this point). The conclusion was that her old school had to put her on secondment to her new school, which meant they still had to pay her wage, but without the benefit of her work (Justice 1, Injustice 0).

The old school stalled on paying her, but with the advice of her new, friendly colleagues, she got a teaching union involved and pretty soon they had to cough up (Justice 2, Injustice 0). At the end of a few months her old school grudgingly gave her a qualification she'd been working for (Justice 3, Injustice 0) and she was free to work for her new school (Justice 4, Injustice 0), who offered her a job. Later, over Christmas drinks in the pub, one of her new colleagues just happened to mention someone who had previously applied for her job. He'd been turned down without even an interview. The bloke? Mr Christian-persecuter (Justice 5, Injustice 0).

Finally, God finished the whole job off with a little flourish and a twinkle: the brand new head of department at her old school was a fully paid-up, self-confessed, up-for-it Christian (Justice wins the day).

Injustice lives near me

If we think injustice happens only on the big screen, between nations or in well-publicised cases, we're wrong. Injustice flourishes in homes, schools, factories, offices and basically wherever there are human beings. Why? Yeah, it's that old chestnut: fallen world. But if that were the whole story, it'd be a pretty depressing picture. Luckily, it isn't. Check out any of the Bible verses above and you'll find a God who is passionately concerned about justice, passionately against oppression of any kind and eager to get on the case of justice in his beautiful, but spoiled, world.

Chapter four

Just the odd talent?

OK, so we're becoming convinced that justice is good, true, honest, noble and something we generally want to spend a portion, at least, of our lives trying to bring about. What now? Chances are, if you're into justice in any way, you will check out some of the people down the ages who have likewise shown a passion for the old setting-things-right game. Maybe that will include people like the slave-law reformer, Wilberforce, or I-have-a-dream Martin Luther King. Perhaps Gandhi walking the simple path of peaceful resistance inspires you in your crusade against injustice (even if it just means not getting into a fight with the lads in Year 11 who are tormenting a mate of yours). Maybe you can think of others who have made valuable contributions to life, health and hope over the last few millennia on planet earth.

Such reading is good, even vital, to feed our justice-hungering hearts. But what if you're not the world's greatest speaker? What if you can't mobilise the masses to march on government and bring reform? What if you don't have the talent, the ideas and the inspiration these people had? Well, fret not. There are many ways to bring justice to the world and God is not limited by our talents, only by our lack of willingness to roll up our sleeves and get our hands (whatever they're good at doing) dirty.

Fantasy justice league

I used to have this fantasy, when a charity I was involved with was having a run-in with a multinational over its baby-milk policy, that I would be the one to negotiate a high-level meeting with them. They would come into the charity buildings bristling with hostility. We'd fix up a meeting with other high-level movers and shakers in the organisation. We'd sit round a table in a meeting room discussing their evil, unjust way of working. They would be moved by our words and our attitude of mercy. They would realise the enormity of the mistakes they had made. One by one they would break down weeping, confessing their wrongdoing. We would assure them that it would be OK, that all they needed to do was to change. They would be grateful for our advice, humbled by our generosity in inviting them to talk to us. They would leave, shaking our hands and promising to reform. Everyone would be amazed. God would applaud.

But fantasy it strictly was. What I failed to take into account in this little fantasy of mine is my absolute inability in this area. Even as I'm being handed my first cup of coffee at the start of a meeting my eyes are beginning to glaze over and it takes a superhuman effort even to nod, let alone to stay engaged. Fortunately God is a lot more aware of my limitations than my imagination seems to be (though I like to think it amuses him). I thank God I've actually had jobs that contribute to the bigger justice picture and which, amazingly, have used some of the talents God so generously doles out to each one of us. (And by the way, may the networkers and policy-changers live long and prosper – the work of justice needs you, too.)

> If I had, literally, to feed the poor, I'd be saying: do you want white bread or brown? One slice or two? Low-fat marge or butter? As, at the other end of the line in the refugee camp, another person drops dead. This kind of hands-on practicality doesn't come easy to me, as my friends and family will be only too eager to tell you. Happily, there is more to feeding the poor than being the next Jamie Oliver.

To push this point further, a friend of mine is a talented film- and video-maker. He lectures in visual arts at a highly rated university department and, in his spare time, whips off graphics for mainstream TV. I was lucky enough to be involved in collaborating with him over a video. Paul was talented, experienced and had a high level of expertise. He helped make a video that sold out, went round the world to Australia and got Christians talking about issues like HIV/AIDS, UK homelessness, war and refugees. At the end of an exhilarating and highly creative few months, Paul turned to me and (unbelievably) said, 'What use is the stuff I do? Shouldn't I be out there feeding the poor? How does what I do help anyway?' My jaw, I have to say, kind of hit the floor.

Now you could call it post-production blues and simply write it off, but I think Paul was making a point lots of us feel when we get into justice issues. Namely, 'Here are all these heroic people making a clear difference to people's lives,' (Mother Teresa's name crops up a lot at this point), 'but I don't do that'. And therefore, the argument goes, either a) 'God thinks I'm not much cop' and/or b) 'I will just have to bow out of this particular round of justice-making. Thank you and good night.'

Manufactured justice

Now call me naïve, but I don't think God is looking for a whole bunch of Mother Teresas. If he was, surely there would be a Mother Teresa Clone Factory (McMomT's perhaps?) out there somewhere, churning out strange-looking people (men included) wearing blue and white striped nun habits and talking in Bengali, like some weird version of a doll factory from a Tim Burton film. OK, I'm exaggerating, but you get my point, don't you? God, creative (seventy-thousand-species-of-trees-creative) God, doesn't need us all to be doing the same thing.

By the way, I asked Paul, 'What would happen if just one person with the same kind of skills and talents as Mother Teresa watched the video we'd made, was inspired and decided to devote their life to bettering the lot of humanity?'

It's a good argument to use whenever people are talking about how few people come to their church/sign up for events/sign up for charity magazines/programmes to go abroad. All it takes is one person. One Gandhi. One Martin Luther King. One person with a heart for the poor. Jesus went around speaking to the crowds, but loads of his miracles are a one-to-one affair. One person. And, if we're talking Mother Teresa by the way, she had the exact same attitude. Apparently when someone asked her, 'How do you feed so many people?', she replied, 'One at a time.'

But I'm not creative!

And it's not just about being creative. Let's consider other possibilities for a moment. If you're into maths, you could be a logistician in a disaster situation or a charity accountant (how do you think all those refugee feeding camps get paid for?) or do the books in a mission hospital. If you're a scientist, you could advise poor farmers on how to get a better crop yield to feed their family or community. Into French? How does going to Cameroon in Africa grab you? What about biology? Everywhere in the world needs doctors and many places don't have them. Like mixing with other people? All charities need volunteers, people who love to be with others and help out. Maybe you think you're no good at anything? Chances are, that isn't true. I know someone who loves filing, sorting out admin, helping keep track of what information is where. The whole team in the charity where she works would fall apart without her help.

> Take a moment right now to list any skills or talents you have. Just yours. Now think about ways those skills and talents could be used in the context of caring for the poor and justice. Get excited about what you can do and don't think about what you can't. It's as simple as that.

Eye, eye, ear, ear

Ultimately, we have no reason to feel inferior, no reason to discount others or ourselves. Equally we have no reason to get arrogant and feel better than anyone else. We are in this game together. Paul has this totally right when he says we're like bits of a body. Some of us are ears, some eyes, some arms, some legs, one or two might be feet and your best mate could even be nasal hair. What we do and what we're good at doing is going to look different from what other people do, but that's OK. We can still make justice and so can they. Our only job is, with the help of God, to figure out which bit we are and then get on with being it the best we can, caring about justice, the poor and God's world.

Just hope you're not the bum cheek…

Chapter five

Stickability

When it comes to justice, there isn't some genetically enhanced breed of super-Christian, some Premier-League David Beckham-style hero, who effortlessly curves the ball into the top right corner and takes the crowd's glory, while the rest of us are still in the sixty-third minute, gasping with a terrible stitch and about to miss an open goal. It's a little-known and even less advertised fact that the only thing that sets apart the wannabes from the world-changers is one word: perseverance.

> **I have to be honest and say perseverance doesn't exactly light my fire.**

In fact, perseverance is the kind of thing that brings me out in cold sweats. The word itself brings back little-cherished memories of cross-country runs in the driving rain by busy roads or double maths homework on logarithms (though maybe that did veer into sadism).

So why's it such a big deal? Why does the Bible major on perseverance big-time and what exactly does it mean?

Well, the dictionary defines it this way:

'continued steady belief or efforts, withstanding discouragement or difficulty'.

Believing it and doing it

It's interesting that even the dictionary makes a link between belief and action, belief and effort. It's not a million miles away from what the Bible has to say. Moses, we are told, persevered because of 'he whom he saw' – God. So, one of the keys to perseverance, to having more stickability than a shiny new bit of Velcro, is believing in something (or someone). If we really deep down believe in God and that God cares about justice, the chances are that when the discouragement and difficulties come, we'll have a stronger chance of keeping going.

When resistance comes

When I first got into the whole justice 'n' lifestyle issue I wasn't really into the Christian thing (yet). It was my second year at university and I'd started to read the Bible, but it didn't make a lot of sense to me. I just combined it with my usual college socialising. I did join the Green Party, because some little echo of faith in me was whispering that the world was important and people are important and so is creation. It was really interesting being in that Green Party – we picketed a multinational over their controversial farming policies and sent people off to the wholefood café round the corner. It was a good laugh and I felt a lot of joy doing it.

Then I became a full-on-again Christian. It was great. I loved it. But that sense of the world and creation being important never left me. I assumed every other Christian would feel the same way. It was my first big disappointment. It was my first 'discouragement and difficulty' and the first test of whether I'd keep a steady belief in the issues I felt strongly about. Luckily I met a couple of radical, long-term Christians, who kept on encouraging me.

Out of the university Christian Union, which seemed to tolerate me in a 'never mind, she's a new convert' kind of way, I found myself in a happy-zappy-clappy old church. It was great. It was exciting. It was biblical. They cared about the poor. Fantastic. Here, I thought, is home. Here I am among like-minded individuals.

So I did my usual rabbiting on about life, the universe and our place as Christians in it. I talked human rights. I talked persecuted Christians. I talked environment. I actually cared about politics. Then one day one of the key church people told me that people tried to avoid me; they wanted out; they couldn't, didn't want to and, so the underlying argument went, shouldn't have to put up with me going on about justice and human rights.

To say I was shocked would be an understatement.

> **Maybe I was a social justice bore? Who knows? Maybe
> I did say things that made people uncomfortable.
> Maybe, hey, I needed to get out more, chill out a bit.
> But what that comment did was shut me up.**

Overcoming opposition

For a few months at least, I wasn't sure what to think. Did Christians no longer believe in the importance of human rights and social justice? I was confused. So how did I get over what was said? This probably makes me sound holier than I actually am, but I did go deeper in God. I prayed. I read my Bible. And somehow, slowly, I realised again that justice is completely at the heart of God. I realised that justice never disappears from God's agenda. I realised that God's approval was the most important thing. I realised that it is OK to feel strongly about something and to talk about it and then to leave the rest up to God. Rather than breaking my belief in justice (though for a while it was touch and go), my belief went underground for a while, then came out stronger. Discouragement and difficulties will come, but my job is just to persevere. And so is yours.

> **Chances are, as we mature and grow, we'll all face
> stuff like this. Situations where we're opposed, put
> down, stressed out, frustrated and confused.**

On the plus side, discouragement and difficulties don't usually last. We can try to use them constructively, one of the best ways to beat something bad. As well as learning more about justice, I learnt more about God too, like about his protection, shelter and gentleness. It wasn't an easy time, but it wasn't a wasted time.

Get God involved

Also, we need to remember that God can take – and wants to take – our suffering, our difficulties and our frustrations. When we feel burdened by what we hear (or what we don't hear, like encourage- ment or help), we should never feel we have nowhere to go. We can pray. We can figure out if we were wrong and maybe, too, where we were right. We can forgive. We can move on. And we can keep a steady belief, like Moses, with our hearts and minds fixed on Jesus, our friend, who joyfully makes justice wherever he goes.

Cancel that job lot of lipstick

Along with perseverance goes the idea of the long haul. The unglamorous life. How many times do you think Mother Teresa was filmed compared to the number of times she fed a hungry child, washed a sick man's sores, emptied a dying woman's bed pan? Justice-making is not a career for flash-in-the-pan wannabes. It's not just about cocktail parties at Number 10 and Versace jeans in the AIDS ward. More likely, it's clearing up the dirty needles, the syringes, the used nappies in the refugee camps. It's comforting the parent when their third child dies of diarrhoea. It's attending endless meetings in airless rooms in the hope that debt can be reduced for the poorest countries of the world.

And who does it? Some super-breed of humans? No. They're normal people. People like you and me. People who laugh, cry, have families, fall out with friends. People who eat takeaways and watch soap operas, catch buses and pay bills. People who get tired, frustrated, angry and upset. People you wouldn't recognise if you walked down the street next to them. Ordinary Joe and Joanna Bloggs. People who believe and do something.

From dreaming to doing

I have to be honest: left to my own devices, my life would be a series of schemes, fads and half-finished ideas. However, God looked down from his super-deluxe sofa in heaven (they will have them, believe me, in a triumph of comfort over taste) and said, 'Yeah, now Helen, I think she needs to learn some perseverance. Let's send a few little life-lessons along to help her out.' Sure, there's nothing wrong with innovation. God innovates and creates with the best of them (well, he *is* the best of them) but innovation without application equals nothing. Zero. Zilch. Even the best inventions, the best ideas, have to make it out of your head or off the A3 layout pad and into reality.

Genesis 1 (not)

Imagine Genesis 1 rewritten...

Now God thought about creating earth, but really he preferred just to dream about it. When he did get round to it, maybe he'd create some nice light. Yeah, light would be good and then he could create night, too, which would be equally cool. God started thinking about all the pretty shades of light he could create and how it might look good if he could create a substance called water and maybe shine light through big, white and grey fluffy things he thought he might get round to making, called clouds.

'Wow, that would be pretty,' he imagined. But, as eternal time clicked noiselessly by towards the end of what would have been the first day, he thought, 'All that dreaming has certainly tired me out. I think I'll have a little nap.' And God fell gently asleep in the great void that was.

God awoke on what would have been the second day and thought a bit more about this water substance and how versatile it could be. Hey, maybe he could suspend it and call it 'sky'. Maybe he could also use this water to create snow and ice, rain and rivers, seas and lakes. Maybe it would be really useful later on to a vague idea he had called 'animal' and 'human'.

Again the ageless hands of eternal time ticked on and God came to the end of what would have been the second day. He closed his eyes and water and sky remained just another good idea.

Then the third-day-that-might-have-been came round. God stretched and yawned and thought, 'What can I dream up today?'

And lo, God dreamt up land and plants and trees and food. From oaks and elms to bracken and rhododendrons. He created savannahs and deserts and great rolling open plains and small dinky valleys – at least in his imagination. He made green grass, yellow sand, red dust and brown clay. There were apples and pears, mangoes and pineapples, to name just a few of the nutritious things he'd pencilled in as fruit, hanging off something that might become known as trees.

So, the third day passed in a blur of imaginative creating (if not actual creating) and then the fourth (which saw God's dreaming taking in special pinpricks of light at night called 'stars', a big hot fireball called 'sun', moon to light the night-darkness, winter, summer, spring, autumn, birthdays, Christmas and Easter).

Along rolled the fifth day and God was happily dreaming up trout, eel, whales, sharks, dolphins, jellyfish, stingrays, sea anemones and frogs, along with crows, ravens, rooks and blackbirds. That was just the 'black' section of bird creation – hummingbirds came after a little energy rush after a particularly tasty lunch. It was exciting, even if it was just a dream.

Finally, on what would have been day six, God looked around at everything he had created, the full A–Z from aardvark to zebra, and he saw that it was good. Or rather, that it would have been good, because actually it was still all in God's head. It was still a dream. In actual fact, nothing existed at all. Not one thing.

It may be extreme, but you get the point? If we only dream, if we only imagine, if all our excitement stays only in our head and the passion only in our heart, nothing happens in our messy, messed-up beautiful universe.

We have to dream, yes, but we also have to do something.

When wisdom kicks in

There'll be tough times. There'll be suffering. There'll be opposition and the mystery of things-not-quite-working-out-as-we'd-planned. There'll be times when we wonder, 'What's the point?', when we doubt whether we're doing the right thing. There'll be times, sometimes quite long times, when we'll want to give up or just feel really bored. Sometimes God, in mysterious wisdom, will call us not to the nations of the world or mass evangelism or to world-changing politics, or even simply to touching the life of one person, but only to this: patient enduring. But there is a reward.

'To those who overcome, I will give the right to eat from the tree of life, which is in the Paradise of God.' (Revelation 2:7)

There is joy now for making and caring about justice. There is the total privilege of a relationship with God. There are definite glimpses of a new world order breaking out, made up of justice and harmony. It's this blissed and blessed-out state of affairs that will win in the end, however bad it seems to get along the way.

So, keep on steadily believing and you'll get there. You too will see the hummingbird, but you've got to do something.

Dictionary a-go-go

The dictionary defines justice this way:

'the quality of being morally right and fair'.

It also has a special Christian definition of perseverance which means 'staying in a state of grace before death'. Without delving too deeply into this gem of an idea, it's worth remembering that even in justice we need to steer clear of obligations, shoulds and have-to's – grace and God's love are our motivation. Justice-making comes out of knowing God and knowing he loves us, not out of some cold list of rules and regulations to which we must rigidly stick.

'We love because he first loved us.' (1 John 4:19)

Justice always comes out of love – knowing God loves us, loves the world and loves justice.

Chapter six

Living a balanced life

I saw a documentary once about a bloke who was doing amazing work in Calcutta. He was feeding the hungry, visiting the sick, caring for orphans – all the biblical stuff that should, all things being equal, ensure him a hearty slap on the back from the Lamb of God himself when time stands still on the great clock face of eternity.

Problem was: he wasn't a Christian. Or rather, he used to be a Christian, but wasn't any longer. As he confessed to the fact that he no longer believed, you really could see the pain in his eyes and hear it in his voice. 'Why? Why do you no longer believe?' asked his interviewer. 'All this,' said the man, gesturing to the hordes of dirty, malnourished street children surrounding him. 'How could a God allow so much suffering?'

> **The man was a 24/7 saint, but without any faith that he had a 24/7 God.**

Watching him, I felt sadness, but his story is not unique. Time and again we hear of or even meet people who have been totally involved in doing 'good works' for God, but who now are disillusioned, cynical, even ill, as a result. Our culture has a word for it: burnout. And this chapter is written to help you avoid it, cos it ain't pretty.

Avoiding burnout

Burnout comes about often because people don't live a balanced life. Their passion for justice, for the poor, for human rights or whatever, becomes the overriding object of their lives, almost an obsession. Rather than applauding it, we should be wary.

It's all too easy in the justice game to get into a guilt mentality ('If I don't do this, people are going to suffer, even die') or into obligations ('I should do this. I'm a Christian'). We can place unrealistic burdens on ourselves that, quite frankly, aren't of God.

So, what's the antidote? Well, I find the story of Jesus at the Pool of Siloam intriguing. Here is the Healer of all Time, the man who will, one day soon, save the entire world, and he is walking in amongst a bunch of desperate, chronically sick people.

Now, according to the Jewish belief at the time, an angel would descend from heaven and stir the waters of the pool. When that happened, if you were lame or infirm or downright sick, you would try to get into the water first. Forget polite British queuing. Forget, 'no, no, but after you, I insist!' Forget dignity and putting other people first. Those who made it to the swirling waters of the pool stood as good a chance as any to get better, get well and, in short, pick up their mats and walk.

So what does Jesus do? Set up a little booth and say, 'This way please, form an orderly queue on the left?' Do a little training session with his disciples then go in for a spot of practical laying-on-of-hands healing?

Maybe he decides to hang out there for a couple of days, building up these people's self-esteem, and, at the end of a little one-to-one quality time, to rebuke their sickness and heal them all. End of story. End of Pool of Siloam (sorry: this pool is closed due to lack of sickness). After all, Jesus could. Elsewhere, we are told, they brought all the sick to him and he healed every one of them.

But does he do this? No.

He goes to one man, one man who isn't shuffling his way down to the pool edge. After a little discussion and in the most unshowy, non-'come to the front of the stage those of you who have been healed' kind of way, Jesus simply makes him better. Why just one person in this sea of suffering?

Has Jesus got compassion fatigue?

I don't think so. Rather, I think the clue lies in these words: I do only what I see my Father doing. Jesus was in a relationship with his father, God. He did only what his Father was doing: no more and no less. The exciting thing is, we can imitate this (believe me, it's one of the easier things to imitate about Jesus' life).

We can stay in a relationship with God and, learning to be obedient, we can do only what God is doing and wants to do. We can keep a balanced life this way. Remember, God loves us, so we're not listening to the advice of someone who is a slave-driving tyrant. God is gentle and kind and that's the style of advice we'll get from him.

> So top tip numero uno for living a balanced life: stay in a relationship with God. Be prepared for God to say, 'No, I don't want you to do that.' Allow God to be more than a God of justice, because he is more than that. Say also, a God of laughter, a God who loves parties, a God of silence, a God of creation, a God of time-just-spent-hanging-out-with-mates. Be happy to chill with God, as well as to do the big stuff.

Live within your limits

How else can we avoid burnout? Well, realising our limitations is definitely one of them. Just as we are beginning to get our head round using our own talents and being who we were created to be, so we can realise that we have limitations. We need to sleep. We need to eat. We need space. We need rest. We need relaxation.

I am cheered that large parts of the Old Testament (at least in my mind!) are full of God creating rest (Genesis), creating parties, creating time off and creating holidays. 'Party and make others party' seems to be a much-ignored motto of God. It is deeply heartening to me to see that God declares 'solemn feast days' (by solemn, I don't think he means you can't have a laugh – rather, it shows his seriousness that we should take time out) and entire years off (Sabbath years or Years of Jubilee).

So eager is God to make us rest, he makes a law to do so. Without getting into the whole Sunday-trading argument, we do need to take this part of God's character and wisdom seriously. The Psalms tell us that God gives sleep to those he loves – what a result!

I love sleeping. I'm like the kid who in an advert once said 'I love my bed'! It's a joy to realise that God perhaps isn't calling me to all-night, every-night intercession for the world and its needs, but instead is fluffing up my pillows and saying, 'Take a nap.'

If you don't believe me, check out the story of Elijah (1 Kings). Elijah in 1 Kings 19 is what our culture would call 'burnt out'. He's knackered. He's just confronted a whole load of evil and corrupt priests, called down a miracle and beaten the powerful propehts of Baal. Elated? No, he's had enough.

'Let me lie down and die,' he begs God. He's had enough. So what does God do? Give him a severe telling-off? Say it's cos he hasn't been to church recently that he's so weak? Tell him to snap out of it and think of others? No.

God looks at this prophet he loves and sends him – no, not a vision to reinspire and invigorate him, but some food and sleep. Eat and sleep, says God. When you're ready, we'll talk.

> **So top tip number two for living a balanced life is this: take care of yourself. Eat. Rest. Sleep. And remember, if guilt threatens to kick in, the job advert for Saviour of the world closed about two thousand years ago, following a successful appointment. So there's no point trying to fill it.**

Honest to God

We're not done with Elijah just yet. Let's pick up the story where we left off. Elijah goes to Mount Sinai. Not cos he's some climbing nut, I suspect, but rather because this is a place he's heard God before, somewhere he knows he can go and hear the voice of the Lord.

Then God sends some pretty big, powerful natural phenomena: an earthquake, a hurricane and a fire. Just the stuff of prophecies, you might think, but was God in any of it? No. What was God in then? God was in 'a still, small voice' or, as one Bible translation puts it, 'a gentle whisper'. The Gentle Whisper asks Elijah what he's doing on the mountain and Elijah replies:

'I have been very zealous for the Lord God Almighty. The Israelites have rejected your covenant, broken down your altars, and put your prophets to death with the sword. I am the only one left, and now they are trying to kill me too.' (1 Kings 19:14)

> **Roughly speaking, Elijah tells God he's done a load of hot stuff for him; he's stood up for God, but he feels alone, really alone, and people are trying to kill him. What do we expect God to do?**

Tell Elijah not to be so self-pitying? Reply, 'But I didn't expect any less from you. After all, you say you believe in me.' No, the Gentle Whisper confides in Elijah all that is going to happen. He reassures him that he's not the only one who cares, as well as telling him where he can find someone to help him and eventually take on his job! Result!

So what can we learn from this to avoid burnout? We can learn that it's OK to be honest with God, to tell him when it's hard, or tough, when we feel alone. We can tell him when we feel like we just can't or don't want to do it any more, without fear of any kind of nasty rebuke or a millennium of detentions for 'not trying hard enough' or 'not answering the call'. In fact it's just the opposite: we can expect gentleness.

We can expect God to bring practical solutions to problems we face (Elisha to help out). We can expect God to change our perspective if it needs changing (7,000 other people cared like Elijah did – he wasn't alone after all) and we can expect God to encourage us by telling us what's going to happen.

> So top tip number three: be honest with God when
> it feels hard, tough or you've just had enough.
> Let God be gentle with you and be prepared to find
> him as much, if not more, in the stillness and quiet
> as in the big, loud stuff.

Still feeling weary? Take time out

Whatever stage of life we're at, God knows and understands. He knows and understands what it's like to feel under pressure and he also gets it when you're feeling stressed cos you think you're just not doing enough good 'Christian' stuff or when you've taken on so much good 'Christian' stuff there's no time in your life for anything else.

Why else would he say:

'Come to me, all you who are weary and burdened, and I will give you rest. Take my yoke upon you and learn from me, for I am gentle and humble in heart, and you will find rest for your souls. For my yoke is easy and my burden is light.' (Matthew 11:28–30)

If we really begin to feel burdened by what we're doing, we need to take some serious time out. It's never a cop-out. Major Christians down the centuries have stressed the need for a lifestyle that takes in chilling out. Jesus himself took his disciples away for a little breathing space when things were getting too much and that certainly hasn't changed by the twenty-first century.

Listening to Jesus

Whether we're trying to avoid burnout or recovering from it, let's get up close 'n' personal to Jesus and his words, because they are what we need to hear.

So what is Jesus really saying? First, if we're weary and burdened, we can go to him. 'Come to me,' he says. Elijah went to God and it doesn't change by the time we get to the New Testament.

What you could do is physically go to (or stay in) a place you know you have heard God before, where you feel comfortable. (If you're tired and stressed, it usually isn't a time to strike out. You need reassurance.)

Pray and tell God you're responding to his invitation to come to him, cos you're tired out and stressed. Allow yourself to rest and allow Jesus to give you rest – don't try to fill the gaps with something to do. If you're feeling worried or hyped up, ask God to fill you with his peace. Remember, you're first and foremost a human *being*, not a human doing.

Next, you could look at your life and ask yourself questions like:

What is making me so tired?
What is making me feel like I'm carrying something heavy?
Am I doing stuff that I'm not sure God gave me to do?
Have I taken on stuff because I thought I should?

When you've identified what it is that's making you so weary (if you feel it's just your whole life, then that's fine too!), chat it over with God in prayer.

You could ask him to show you if it's his burden, his yoke you're carrying, or a heavier thing of your own making. If it's becoming clear it isn't what God wants for you, ask him to take it away and show you what you need to do to lay it down.

Maybe this will involve talking to other people, asking to be removed from commitments you've got. It may seem hard at first, but they'll probably appreciate your honesty and it may even help them to live a more balanced life, if they need to. If you need courage, then ask God for that too.

Be prepared for Jesus to take anything away if it isn't his yoke on your shoulders. Enjoy the lightness! Then again, if God does reassure you it's his yoke you're carrying, ask him to refresh you and give you new strength.

Next, listen to Jesus say, 'I am gentle and humble of heart.' A lot of stress comes simply from misplaced ambition. Jesus' antidote and cure is gentleness and humility. It comes back to 'the one' factor. Are you happy sometimes for your life just to touch one person, rather than the crowds or the world? Are you happy for your life to look small and insignificant, if this is what God wants? Let God free you from ambitions that aren't his for your life and begin to discover the joy that comes from humility and gentleness.

Lastly, believe it when Jesus says he wants to give your soul – your true you – rest. It is possible to work and still experience a sense of rest. It is possible to carry a burden and take a yoke that are both easy and light – and it's what Jesus wants for you. Ask God to show you what his will is, his good, pleasing, perfect and restful will for your life. Then say a simple yes to it. To no more and no less than what your loving God wants for you.

If you find any of this hard, just keep on talking to and being honest with God. You'll get there. The Gentle Whisperer will help you – and you will still be living a life of love and justice. It just might be easier than you thought it should be!

Chapter seven

Year of Jubilee

Why not declare a Year of Jubilee like in Leviticus 25? A real justice year in your own life? Doesn't matter if it isn't January; you can start this calendar at any time. You don't have to do it all, just the bits that really jump out at you. Put any of these ideas into practice and you'll begin to live a justice-loving life. And, what's more, you'll love your own life more too, even when you have to persevere through the tough bits, cos you'll be living with a purpose and a sense of your destiny and that can't be bad.

January

Be joyful in everything you do, because God pours out joy on those who love justice. Join like-minded others. Jump into God's love – it'll keep you refreshed and loving God's world. Jail-break: set people free with the truth about your justice-loving God.

February

Feast – open wide your arms, heart and house, showing that God has no favourites. Have fun with friends, family and the forgotten (maybe a neighbour who never gets out). Be festive in frigid February. Favour God's friendship. Reach out to the friendless – they are not excluded from the justice of God. Make sure you are trying to fast from injustice forever. Fuel others' desire for God and for justice. Be fearless, even if you feel scared confronting wrongdoing. Fulfil your dreams for a better world, right where you are now.

March

Make yourself available to God – how does he want to establish justice through you? Make waves. Mingle with other justice-lovers: they'll inspire you and keep you going. Mangle your vices – get rid of bad habits, they just weigh you down. Make yourself heard – maybe there's a local issue you can and want to speak up on? Make yourself listen – who's not being heard who should be? Meditate on God's words – choose verses and stories that will meet your longing for justice. Remember, God cares about justice just as much as, if not more than, you. Make a manifesto – what do you really believe? Is justice on your list? Make room – for God, for others. Meddle in injustice. Munch fair-trade chocolate and bring down unfair global trade systems (if not your size in jeans…).

April

Argue with God – Abraham did. You can too. Where is God not seeming to act and where do you want him to? Adventure into uncharted territory – be bold, justice could break out anywhere, anyhow, or anytime. Anticipate change – keep dreaming of the way things could be and should be. Agitate for something new, whether that's waving a placard or going to see your form tutor about the way someone's being treated wrongly. Attempt what's on your heart for justice – even if you seem to fail. What matters to God is that you tried. Who knows what the eventual result will be? Advertise God, the lover of justice, by getting a reputation for it yourself. Ally yourself with goodness. Act righteously. Add love to every attitude, including your just desires. Art – show God's love of justice in pictures, not just words. Allow God close. Allow weakness – you may not get it right and remember other people won't too. That's where mercy and humility come in. Appreciate God, others and yourself – they may want justice just as much as you do, so don't shut them out.

May

Model yourself on your just God. Find Jesus in the misunderstood. Find out what God's up to and do it. Live with meaning. Mean well.

Who are your mentors? Read a biography of someone who inspires you to love justice – for example Martin Luther King or Mahatma Gandhi. Mystery – live with the unsolved; live with the fact that sometimes in some places injustice and oppression continue, even after your best efforts, but remember it's not the end of the story. Mature and trust God – he needs to be involved in your justice-making too. Make time alone with Jesus – sometimes he will just want to love you and be with you.

June

Jive to God's rhythms in your life – what makes you dance, sing and celebrate? When justice is achieved, 'the righteous shout for joy'. Jerusalem, Jakarta, Jalalabad, Johannesburg: jet-set your prayers and pray for justice all over the place. Jump-start your life: recharge your batteries on God's love. Jack in the pessimisim – it'll all work out, even if it takes time.

July

Journey for others – go the extra mile for those who need justice, whether that's writing a letter to a prisoner to encourage them or adding your name to an injustice-crushing petition. Don't judge – it's a heavy burden. You don't know what work someone may be doing behind the scenes for your cause. Journal – keep one, of what happens. You may be surprised – God promises to bring justice quickly. Join heaven in praising the God who wants justice established on the earth. Jubilee – let your own debtors off, the people who have done you wrong, and forgive. Jugular – go for it. Speak your mind in love.

August

Anchor – be one for those in the stormy sea of injustice. Let God be yours as you come close to those who are suffering. Allow God's arms around you. Be in awe of God – he is capable of much more than you could ever imagine or ask for. Love the alien – make sure you don't oppress anyone around you, whether by what you think, say, do or don't do. Apply modesty to your life and avoid affluence – bowing out of the consumer game could mean fewer sweatshops, less child labour and fewer riches for the world's unscrupulous. Anti-freeze your heart – let God's love be your lifeblood. Alleviate suffering by doing what you can, not what you can't. Be an activist. Abbreviate your life to one word – love. Justice flows out of a heart that loves. Annoy the unjust. Don't worry about adversaries – let God deal with the opposition.

September

Shovel – do God's dirty work. It may take effort to stay with justice, but stick it out. Stubbornly love. See Jesus in others – who else is working for justice? Secret – what's God gently whispering in your heart? Making justice doesn't have to be big. It can be as small as giving someone a hug or nodding when they make a point in class. Space – find it. Let go of what's surplus in your life – chuck out what you don't need. Seek freedom; seek peace. Get silly – it's OK. This justice business is sometimes serious, but that doesn't mean you should give up smiling. Serve God and other people. Submit to God. Struggle honestly – some days you won't have the answers, the tough times will come. Stick it out – there are better days ahead. Sabbath – get rest in your life. Make sure you stay balanced and don't burn out. Simply be – it's not all about what you do. Shamefaced – do good to your enemies. It just might make them think twice about what they're doing. Sanctify your days with prayer.

October

Open out – be expansive. Who can you include in your justice-making? Don't let it be a solo affair. What will you have given when you're old? Appreciate the elderly and wisdom that recognises that justice will outlive oppression. Embrace otherness, different cultures – don't be unjust in your attitudes. Be an optimist – share hope. Don't go overboard – be gentle. Be original – remember it's your talents God wants to use, not someone else's. Who is an outcast? Justice-lovers invite them in.

November

Be naked with God, really real. Get down to the nitty-gritty, how you really feel (just like Elijah, don't feel the need to have any religious pretending before such a close friend). Never say never – do what's necessary to let God's loving justice loose in the neighbourhood. Nudge God to get involved. No – accept God's limitations on you. If you aren't going to Sudan to shelter the home-less, live with it. You'd hate it if it wasn't the real God-created you, anyway. Love the nobodies and show that God's justice isn't limited. Admit your need – whether that's for justice, rest, sleep, help, whatever. Know that nothing separates you from God's love.

December

Dream of a world where there is no injustice. If you can't, read Revelation and ask God to make it real in your mind and heart. Disbelieve the hype – the enemies may look bigger than they really are. Dove of peace – give it a home. Delight in God's love. Dare to be different – even if you have to stand out from the crowd for the sake of justice, don't worry. You'd be surprised how many people you are secretly inspiring. Don't despair – it's a waste of good energy! Dive into compassionate justice. Deep down, love God. Dread nothing – the Bible tells us to fear no human being. Don't give up doing good. Depend on God – he'll make it real and better than you could have dared hope. Get down with the down-and-outs – they're included in God's plan, too. What's dawning in your life? Do you have ideas of how you could use your skills to further the work of justice? Nurture the ideas till they're strong, then go for it. Difficulties? We all have them. Invite God in. Dare to leave some of it up to God.

> 'He has showed you, O people, what is good.
> And what does the Lord require of you?
> To act justly and to love mercy
> and to walk humbly with your God.'
> (Micah 6:8)

SECTION TWO:

WEALTH

Chapter eight

Money matters

A few years ago, a number of Christians rediscovered the whole Celtic Christianity thing. The Celts were some of the original inhabitants of the British Isles. The way historical people like Aidan, Hilda and Cuthbert had lived out their faith in a pagan culture – with priority given to things like justice, the environment, art and evangelism – was getting a fair proportion of UK Christians pretty excited.

Books on Celtic Christianity and bands like Iona, who were 'Celtic' in their musical style, were popular. In particular, some churches were interested in how their styles of worship and 'doing church' could reflect some of the issues the Celtic Christians had concerned themselves with.

I wonder how many of them got excited by the Celtic love of simplicity?

There's a story of how one Celtic Christian (Aidan) was respected and admired by the king of Northumberland. The king was so impressed by Aidan that he gave him a horse. A horse was a pretty big deal in those days – not just an antidote to sore feet, but a status symbol too. Aidan accepted the horse, only to give it away again almost immediately to a beggar. He believed the beggar to be even poorer than himself and decided to carry on walking everywhere.

> **The story of Aidan clearly shows a Christian who is free from the love of possessions; someone who is free to give when he wants to; someone who doesn't feel bound to have what everyone else has or to climb the ladder of riches or self-importance.**

Aidan was a big deal in the Celtic church – teaching only what he put into practice. He was content to walk everywhere he went. He was content with little and slow.

I saw a documentary on TV once about a band who were evangelists. They went into a school to talk to a group of students about their faith. The programme-makers interviewed various students and teachers after they had met the evangelists to find out their reactions. One concern shared by students and teachers alike was the image the band was putting out. One interviewee said he felt uncomfortable about the cool gear, latest labels and best mobile phones the evangelists had. It was clear that they had expected a more socks 'n' sandals approach. Was this fair?

The evangelists would've defended themselves on the grounds that they were relating to the people they were trying to talk to. They'd probably say that image is a big, big deal in our culture – which it is. Maybe their thinking was shaped by Paul, who said he tried whatever was necessary in order to win over people to Jesus (1 Corinthians 9:18–27).

The evangelists knew that socks 'n' sandals would mark them out as sad, out-of-touch religious people, with little of relevance to say on living life here and now.

But it's a difficult call to make, isn't it?

> **If we want to evangelise the rich and famous, does this mean we need to have plastic surgery, go on expensive holidays and wear designer gear from highlighted head to pedicured foot?**

Is this what Paul meant? Or, more broadly, if we want to have anything to say to people who live in a rich culture, does that mean we have to be rich and live like they do, too? Just how are we meant to feel about money and faith?

Confused church

Church leaders can sometimes seem to be just as confused about money as we are individually. Take this story a friend told me. She was once struggling to pay some extra rent, through no fault of her own. At the time she had started attending a church where the majority of people were quite wealthy.

She found herself in conversation at the end of the service with a man on the 'welcoming team'. He was very pleasant, but when he asked her how she was, she found her eyes welling up with tears as she explained that her landlord was asking her for extra rent which she didn't have. Both she and the man were embarrassed. He quickly wound up the conversation and walked away.

My friend later discovered that this man was very wealthy. Could he have given her some money? Probably. Should he have done? Who can say? What my friend found, however, was that when this man stood up to pray about the needs in the community, when he prayed that new converts would be added to the church, she found it hard to be enthusiastic. Why?

Well, our credibility as Christians, whether we like it or not, is judged as much on what we do and don't do – and that includes our attitude to cash – as on the songs we sing, the prayers we pray and our attitude to our neighbours. (And no, I'm not just talking tithing.)

I'm not saying that this man should automatically have dug deep into his pocket and pulled out a wad of fivers with a flourish, but neither did he offer her comfort. The Bible is realistic about it all:

'What good is it, my brothers, if a man claims to have faith but has no deeds? Can such faith save him? Suppose a brother or sister is without clothes and daily food. If one of you says to him, "Go, I wish you well; keep warm and well fed," but does nothing about his physical needs, what good is it?' (James 2:14–16)

Sorry, no poor people here

We have to ask the question: how open are our churches to the poor? One of the main issues that determine how accessible our churches are, perhaps much more so than whether our church has nice signs outside and a welcoming group, is our attitude to money.

I know of one church which I just can't go to. Is it because the worship is bad? No, it's very good. The preaching, the prayer, the lack of spiritual gifts? Again, all no. Is it because I'm some weird, dodgy troublemaker? (Don't answer that.) No, the simple reason is that I just can't afford it. I just can't keep up.

The impression the church gives – and maybe it isn't aware of it – is that you need money to get involved in any meaningful way. Want to serve in this particular church? Great, but you'll need to go on a weekend away and that will cost you. Want to go to house group? Great, but don't forget to bring the cake or the crisps or the pasta. Want to celebrate a friend's pregnancy? Fantastic, but it'll be embarrassing for them, and you, if you turn up empty-handed.

Is that second-hand?

Maybe I'm at fault, but I would find it tough to invite these people to my house, where the carpet is second-hand, where some of my neighbours are slightly strange, where we eat in the kitchen, nudging the fridge on one side and the cheap shelves on the other, where the decor isn't tastefully co-ordinated in this season's hot colours and we don't have an up-to-the-second stereo turning the tunes.

That isn't to say we can't or shouldn't socialise together as Christians – of course we should. And it's not to say that rich people can't go to church – of course they can and do! Jesus himself hung out with rich people and partied away with the best of them.

But when churches haven't grappled robustly with the issue of money, there is a danger that they may appear to be just that tad exclusive, remaining a church that's attended by the rich, by people who socialise with the rich. The danger arises when you forget that there are people who earn less than £600 a week or for whom a skiing holiday is a distant and unlikely-to-be-fulfilled dream.

And I haven't even asked you whether you think Jesus would have felt comfortable there…

Rich list

One youth group I heard of began to think about this very issue. They looked around at their cool clothes and state-of-the-art mobile phones and started to ask, how would you feel if you wanted to come to this group? What if you came from a family that was struggling to feed itself, let alone wear expensive gear? What if you felt inferior because of what you didn't own and couldn't legitimately afford? Would you still come?

They suspected not, and they were probably right. What's more, such exclusivity – whether it's intended or not – is a long, long, long way away from the early church, where:

'All the believers were together and had everything in common. Selling their possessions and goods, they gave to anyone who had need.' (Acts 2:44,45)

Now that would be a church anyone could feel comfortable in.

It's also not really true to say that there are areas with no poor people. More and more places are a mix of rich, poor and somewhere in-between. Even churches that are in rich areas may have beggars on the street outside – and they can still connect with other groups who are helping poorer people, even if they are a few miles away.

Money, money, money

We seem to have come quite a long way away from the early church, from Aidan, even from Christians in medieval times who regularly turned their backs on their privileged upbringings, all for Jesus. We need to get our heads round this issue of money, both as churches and as individuals. It's evident we live in a majorly materialistic society. The average amount of money spent per person last Christmas was over five hundred pounds, and that's PER PERSON!

On the other side of the fence from desperately consumerist Christians are those who seem to believe we should melt down all our coins and go back to trading wheat and horseshoes. These

Christians seem to believe that God is like a foreign tourist, fumbling with strange coins and asking in a loud, puzzled voice, 'What is this?'

Fishing for cash

We can't avoid money and it would be unrealistic to expect us to. Even Jesus got a fish to spit out a coin when the local council sent their final demand for tax (Matthew 17:27). What we can do is develop an understanding of what the Bible has to say about money, poverty and wealth. The Bible is stuffed with references to money and what our attitude should be towards it, and we're going to check out both the rich and poor side of the coin.

While we do so, let's also remember that the hungry and thirsty, the sick and naked may also be down our streets or in our churches. Let's make sure we care for each other properly, and that includes materially.

Chapter nine

Five-course, five-star

When I was a student in my final year, I remember settling down one evening to the prospect of curry cooked by one of my housemates. Now these curries weren't sumptuous affairs dreamed up in a gastronomic centre of excellence. They weren't dripping in cream with subtly-flavoured and tender chicken, korma-ised within an inch of its life. There was no ice-cold beer in the fridge or poppadoms so crisp they would snap if you so much as sneezed.

No, the curries of which I speak were a mix of raisins (how we came to this I can't remember, but we truly believed raisins were a meat substitute, and therefore, as we were a semi-vegetarian household, offensive to none), yellow rice and – er – not much else. The curries were sticky, stodgy and came fresh out of a plastic bowl in the microwave. On the plus side, they were filling.

So there I was, some post-exam sunny evening in the suburbs of Birmingham, when the phone rang. It was for me. It was a relative I hadn't seen for some years. He wanted to take me out for an evening meal and he'd be at my house in thirty minutes. Now this wasn't just any relative. This guy used to dine with Margaret Thatcher when her business card read '10 Downing Street'. This relative owned a yellow Porsche and sent his wife to Europe for the evening to the opera. Rich? Oh yes.

With just five minutes to spare, I was wearing a (borrowed) skirt, (semi-clean) shirt (the only one without holes), sandals (in place of my regulation trainers), and I'd just about managed to get my hair dry. It didn't feel like me. It didn't look like me. But it was me.

And as my relative roared up in his two-seater yellow Porsche, I waved as though being wined and dined every evening at a five-star hotel is second nature to me. (I don't think he was fooled.)

Two hours later, we had eaten our way through five courses, each revealed with a flourish from beneath a silver dish. My eyes were watering – not simply from gratitude, but more from the price of a thimbleful of dessert wine, which, I had noticed from the menu, cost the equivalent of two whole bottles of wine from the local off-licence. Then my relative peeled one wad of notes from an even bigger wad of notes and the meal was over. (By the way, we did talk about God, at which point I did think this was the kind of evangelism I could handle...)

Rich and Christian?

There are people, the world over, who are very, very rich. We probably know who they are because our culture regularly makes such a big deal about celebrity and riches. Just think of the headlines: Top 100 Richest People! Top 10 Most Powerful Men!

Some rich people hoard their wealth, build their own empires and die, feeling who knows what. Other rich people give money away in grants, set up foundations, and try to better the lot of the world. They're known as millionaire philanthropists – they have a lot of money, but they also give a lot of it away to good causes.

Billionaire Christian businesspeople

When I was a student, I lived within a Creme Egg's throw of Cadbury's at Bournville. Bournville is a beautiful, quiet suburb, full of Tudor-style houses and with a tranquil green, even though it is only a few miles outside the city centre of Birmingham.

Cadbury's was founded by the Cadbury family, who were Quakers. As part of their enterprise, they wanted to build decent houses with gardens for their workers, who otherwise lived in slums. Their business strategy included caring for their employees and especially the poor. That isn't to deny that their business was very successful. But it's intriguing to see a mix of business and ethics working together. Wealth need not imply an absence of God.

> **Being rich carries with it special responsibilities.**

Job was the richest man in his part of the world at the time, and he said to God that he did not believe he had withheld justice from his employees, and if he had, he begged God to show him how (Job 31:13–15).

Job shows us that having great wealth carries with it a responsibility for social concern.

Fair's fair

I think this money/justice thing is beginning to happen, but we can make it happen even more. You see it in the way people are beginning to question where the stuff they buy comes from and how it was produced. The Fairtrade Foundation, with its special symbol, is a visible response to the demand to know that justice has shaped how the stuff we buy got on to our shop shelves. You can see it in the way programme makers and editors send investigative journalists off around the globe. They try to find out how multi-nationals treat the people who produce the goods. These programmes no longer seem too unusual or off-the-wall. Even business consultants are saying that social responsibility is the next big business idea.

In fact, the way goods are produced should be at the forefront of our retail thinking as Christians. We've got so much motivation to ask questions – not least the fact that God passionately cares, too.

Expose slave labour

We should be asking questions like, 'Did the people who produce this get a fair deal? Are they being treated properly? Do they get labour rights? Can they belong to a union? Do they get paid fairly? Are they protected? Is safety adequate?' As part of the planet's wealthy, we cannot divorce money from justice.

Don't believe you're wealthy? If you keep food in the fridge, clothes in a wardrobe, have a roof over your head and a bed to sleep in, you're richer than seventy-five per cent of the world. Never mind if those clothes have labels, that the fridge is designer or the bed is king-size.

So, as part of the world's wealthy, you will want to ask questions about how the people who produce your goods are treated. Those questions say 'I care about people', and we care because God cares.

OK, it's not always easy getting answers to these questions. I remember going to buy a pair of trainers. The shop was packed and the shop assistant kept bringing me the most popular brand name of trainer at the time, which everyone else was happily trying on and buying. I pretended to try them on (at the time, I didn't have the guts to start a major debate about human rights in a shop full of strangers), but I knew journalists were investigating the company that produced the trainers because of the way they treated some of their global producers.

Finally, the shop assistant brought out a pair of trainers by a rival brand name which had a human rights foundation. I snapped them up. They weren't nearly as comfortable, but my conscience was clear.

Does this sound extreme? I hope not (though I really should have hung out for a comfier pair of trainers).

It really is true that, however big and global a corporation is, they are completely relying on you to buy their stuff. No one is standing with a gun to your head commanding you to buy a particular brand.

Yes, there are lots of pressures – like what's the coolest label, who else is wearing it, what does it say about me that I use this brand, not that brand, or even no brand at all – but as Christians, aren't we meant to be courageous as well?

> We should be courageous, compassionate and intelligent enough to know that if a company produces trainers – and doesn't care that a child made them in a sweatshop in dangerous conditions for minimal pay – they are not worth having.

But hey, this isn't a guilt-trip. God doesn't want us to be like those cartoon characters who have dollar bills instead of eyes. Whereas we can get blinded to the nature of money, God has 20:20 clear vision. He knows the reality...

Unreliably well off

One of the reasons God doesn't want us to rely on riches, is that they are unreliable. Check out the stock market any time and you'll see share prices rising and falling like a roller coaster at a theme park. The husband of a friend of mine works in finance. He told me recently that he couldn't believe he used to live on less than £600 a week – a monthly salary for some people. But his company expected him to work an average twelve-hour day. He commutes for an hour a day. And he has a family. A week after telling this story, he was sacked – albeit it with six months' pay and the regulation that he didn't turn up at the company's office again. Such sackings are apparently commonplace in the business he worked for.

Proverbs says: 'Cast but a glance at riches, and they are gone, for they will surely sprout wings and fly off to the sky like an eagle' (Proverbs 23:5).

Sometimes riches come with a price tag that God may say is just too much for us to pay.

The cost of freedom

Another reason why God doesn't want us to get caught up in the riches race is that he values our freedom. Freedom really is something that money can't buy. A new bloke stood up at a charity staff meeting one day to say something on the subject of thankfulness. He began, 'A few months ago, I was earning £1,250 per week. Now I am here. I thank God that he provides.' While half the room was digesting the fact that they were in the presence of someone who had earned more than their monthly wage in one week, I was also thinking, 'Here is a man who is free.'

Put another way, he might well have said, 'Whether I'm on a huge weekly wage or here working for charity, I am in God's hands and that's OK.'

We need to develop this kind of attitude when it comes to cash. Not grabbing and grasping greedily, but accepting with open hands either the bread crust or the tub of caviar that comes from a loving Father, from whom, we are told, 'every good and perfect gift comes.'

If a tub of caviar does come your way, enjoy it. But share it with others. For, if we're rich, God is hoping we'll cheerfully hand out, not miserably hoard.

Nehemiah said, 'Go and enjoy choice food and sweet drinks, and send some to those who have nothing prepared' (Nehemiah 8:10).

I'm rich, so I can afford to give away more? Maybe not.

You would think that the richer you become, the more generous you would become too. Right? Maybe not. Jesus tells a story about this self-same principle.

'Jesus sat down opposite the place where the offerings were put and watched the crowd putting their money into the temple treasury. Many rich people threw in large amounts. But a poor widow came and put in two very small copper coins, worth only a fraction of a penny.

Calling his disciples to him, Jesus said, "I tell you the truth, this poor widow has put more into the treasury than all the others. They all gave out of their wealth; but she, out of her poverty, put in everything – all she had to live on"' (Mark 12:41–44).

Poor and generous

I was once lucky enough to interview a man who worked in the slums in Delhi. A middle-class Indian by birth, he'd turned his back on his privileged upbringing and taken to a life of drugs, living among the slum-dwellers he would later serve. His enduring memory? Their generosity. They, who had so little, would be so quick to give.

Think for a moment about the people in your own life who have been most generous and also perhaps when you were most generous: was it when you/they were loaded or less well off?

Funny, isn't it? For some people, the problem with riches is that the more they increase, the stickier they become. They get harder and harder to let go of and little by little our freedom is eroded.

Sticky money

I used to work with a woman who was my role model and we became very good friends. I found out that she was really into selling antiques at markets and, secretly, she existed for the weekends when she could fulfil this passion. Later on, she let slip that she and her husband had even considered opening an antique shop, visiting shops for sale and considering whether to do it.

When I asked her what was stopping her from fulfilling her dream, she said 'this', meaning her job and her money. She said, 'You get used to a certain lifestyle.' And I'm sure it's true. It's a sad fact that a sofa or wanting to eat out in a restaurant could prevent us from fulfilling our dreams.

Someone told me another story. An older friend of hers had always wanted to live in the country. Life circumstances had brought her to the city, where she raised a family. But suddenly it was possible for her husband to get a job in the part of the country she wanted to move to.

She visited schools with her children and they were accepted for the September term. The next time I caught up with my friend she told me the family hadn't moved. They'd done the sums and realised they couldn't afford a second car, so they weren't going.

I think sticky money is what Jesus talks about when he says you're going to have problems pleasing both your bank account and God. According to Jesus, you just can't go for both things with an equal passion (Luke 16:13).

In fact, money is much further down the importance list than we might think. Check out Proverbs, where it says, 'Better a meal of vegetables where there is love than a fattened calf with hatred.' (Proverbs 15:17)

Five pence or five grand. I'm happy?

Does Jesus then mean we will be poor? Possibly. Does Jesus mean we can't be wealthy and a Christian? I don't think so – though we may have some special responsibilities if we're rich, like the responsibility to be just and generous.

If you're loaded, maybe it's worth considering giving stuff away to people who really need it. Not sure who they are? Pray – God'll soon show you who they are. And hey, how cool to be in a position to help other people!

Jesus isn't naïve about money. He does seem to say, 'beware'. Why? Well, money and the things it can buy can have such a pull for us, hold such sway over us, that the real riches of life (fulfilment, wisdom, contentment, love) may simply pass us by and we may end up hating our lives, however great and cool our possessions or however fat our bank accounts.

I've known what it is to be wined and dined and I've also known what it is to be so broke you have to pray for someone to give you money to pay your rent. I've given money to people stressed about their debts/rent/bills and I've been given money when I've been stressed about mine, too.

In short, like Paul, I have known what it is to be rich and poor. God wants me to be content whatever, because being content is something you can be whether you are rich or poor. Our contentment doesn't need to rely on something as shaky as money.

Stinking rich

Finally, if money isn't wealth, what is? You know how sometimes the Bible really isn't clear about something? Well, luckily on the subject of true wealth, it is. Want to know what is really priceless in God's eyes? It's wisdom.

> 'Wisdom is supreme; therefore get wisdom.
> Though it cost all you have, get understanding.
> Esteem her, and she will exalt you;
> embrace her, and she will honour you.
> She will set a garland of grace on your head
> and present you with a crown of splendour.'
> (Proverbs 4:7–9)

Want to know something even better? It's free. Oh yes. And you can have it – all you've got to do is ask.

> 'If any of you lacks wisdom, you should ask God, who gives generously to all without finding fault, and it will be given to you.' (James 1:5)

Is it worth asking? Well, if they did a richest-man-on-earth-of-all-time survey, I reckon I know who would top it: Solomon. According to the Bible, there's never been anyone richer – he'd make the Beckhams look shabby. But what really made Solomon rich? His wisdom. It's clearly a top gift, and well worth having.

Chapter ten

Being poor

Margaret's story

When I met Margaret she was living in shack K72 in a small settlement of slums on a patch of dry, red earth out in the middle-class suburbs of Nairobi. She was stirring a bowl of boiling water over an open fire and invited me into her tiny hut – a mud structure with a corrugated iron roof. Over a mug of cocoa, which she'd been making for herself and her grandson, Kevin, aged two, she told me her story.

She had lived in a decent house with her husband. But he'd met another woman and decided he wanted nothing more to do with his former family – Margaret, their daughter who was pregnant at the time, and their grandchildren – and so he'd thrown them out.

Since then, Margaret told me, she'd slept on the bare soil floor of the shack, with her family. Neighbours had recently given her the two beds that now filled the hut, along with bags of filthy clothes.

Margaret babysat Kevin, while her daughter did washing for other people, and tried to send Kevin's older brother, aged five, to school. Margaret had a deal going with the teacher that she would pay the school fees (the equivalent of 10p a week) when she could. Education might be the only way out from the kind of grinding poverty that Margaret's family had suddenly found itself in.

Later, I found out that Margaret had been under threat of eviction and had considered killing herself as a way out.

Margaret's story is far from unique.

> All over the world, including in the UK
> (where poverty exists, although it may be much
> more hidden), people struggle to feed, wash,
> clothe and house themselves.

The reasons for poverty are complex, but it's difficult to come away from a situation like Margaret's thinking that this is right, that it is OK for human beings to live like this, while elsewhere in the same city, people are deliberating over whether they are going to have steak or lamb chops for their evening meal.

Rich and poor living together

I saw and felt this even more clearly on a visit to Bombay. It seemed to me that every single street in this hot, dusty mega-city was filled with row upon row of pavement dwellers – people who literally live on the streets, washing their children, scooping rice from stainless steel plates, urinating, cooking over open fires, sleeping, begging.

As the sun set towards the end of one of my days there, we made our way over to reputedly the biggest slum in Asia. Along with the makeshift shelters, people had even built two-storey huts (dangerously without foundations) on a huge stretch of wasteland. There were shops selling everything from vegetables to steel crockery. Carts drawn by oxen moved slowly up wider 'main' streets. Barefoot children scampered over mounds of dry earth and broken glass, flying kites behind them made out of flimsy paper and string.

I was visiting a slum health clinic – a tiny room with a small, creaking fan and lizards running up the walls. It was hard to believe that this one room serviced the needs of all the people who lived in the slum. But what really shocked me, apart from the size of the slum (something like a British town), were the huge great skyscrapers through which the fiery, orange evening sun was now setting.

Someone living there had already told me that Bombay had some of the most expensive property prices in Asia. In fact, accommodation in some of these skyscrapers would cost as much to rent or buy as a penthouse property in Hong Kong.

It was very hard to stomach such absolute poverty coexisting with absolute wealth. I guess it had been made worse by the sight of a rich businessman in his tailored suit roughly pushing aside a barely dressed beggar with his expensive leather briefcase just outside the railway station earlier in the day.

Get motivated

So what was the point of mentioning these encounters? Well, there were several.

> **Sometimes I think it is all too easy to hide our emotions about poverty. We want to calm down our indignation and make our anger decent and acceptable, when what we see is neither decent nor acceptable.**

I'm not talking here about ranting for the sake of ranting or feeling sorry for people, which achieves nothing. I am talking about the purposeful, righteous anger that moves you to act.

What do you feel when you see someone begging in the streets or at the train station? Do you explain it away? Do you say, 'Someone else will look after them, someone else can care for them.' Or do you wonder what you can do? Strong emotions like anger can be a great motivation for getting involved and showing you care.

Passionately caring

An ex-librarian who felt strongly that God was calling her to work with prostitutes – an idea that, quite frankly, deeply scared her – set up a project in Bristol. She had a van that she and other volunteers took out on the streets. They gave out condoms and chocolate and were there for the women to talk to.

Why chocolate? Simply, because the women liked it. They liked to come into the van for a chat and something nice to eat. Then, if a woman needed to go into hospital, the project would provide a nightie and a sponge bag for her. These were simple, small, practical, loving things.

At Christmas, the women and their children were invited to a meal. At each setting on the table, there was a single flower. The project wanted to tell these women that they were still beautiful.

Does it sound like this project is caring about these women? I am convinced that, when I get to heaven, Jesus isn't going to ask me whether I understand global trade figures, GNP, trends in development work or disaster mitigation (useful and good as these things are).

What Jesus will want to know is whether I fed the hungry and thirsty, looked after the sick, visited the imprisoned, gave clothes to the naked and invited in the stranger (Matthew 25).

Jesus talked about caring for people in the parable of the Good Samaritan. It's such a familiar parable, and often used in such guilt-inducing sermons, that it's almost hard to hear anything new or relevant in it. But beyond all the theology and all the finer points, there is one clear, shining truth – care for others.

How we care for people who are poor will require prayer, inspiration, creativity and passion. I can't even begin to answer the question, 'who is my neighbour in the global village?', but I do know that if I don't care when my elderly widowed neighbour can't cook her tea when there is a power cut, that if I don't care when my alcoholic neighbour wants to stop me for a chat, that if I don't care when the slightly strange woman with the scary dog down the road looks to me for a wave and a smile, then I'm not fulfilling the most basic of Jesus' desires – care for others.

Love your neighbour

I wonder what the world would look like if we really looked after people around us? What going overseas has shown me, perhaps most of all, is that it's not so much what you do when you are on a trip overseas that counts, but what you do when you get home.

Although there's a wealth of information telling us which is the poorest country in the world and why, and although we are bombarded with all kinds of images every day from around the world, I wonder if God really didn't mean what he said – look after your neighbour. From Manchester to Mombasa, I wonder how such a simple idea could transform our world.

What would life be like for those slum-dwellers if their wealthy penthouse-dwelling neighbours actually looked down, saw them and wanted to do something for them? What would life be like for Margaret if just one middle-class person came out from their gated house, past their barking guard dogs, and gave her bed linen, kids' toys, towels, food, a job? What would life be like if that rich businessman had given that beggar the time of day, let alone some money or his packed lunch?

Poverty isn't restricted to countries or people groups or even particular bits of our villages, towns or cities. I once walked round a local area with a friend of mine who'd been involved in housing work there. The area had a reputation for wealth, and several celebrities lived within a tiara's throw of where we were. I had assumed that all the Victorian conversion flats we were walking past would be well beyond my financial means, but my friend corrected me.

A large proportion of property belonged to the housing association and council, and it was the same in the next street and the street after that. So, nestling in amongst the Porsche-driving brigade, cheek by jowl with the billionaires, were those who were simply scraping by.

Whether we get to fly to the other side of the world or never leave the place where we were born, we have no excuse not to care about the poor. We could be poor ourselves. How would we want to be treated?

That doesn't mean that we shouldn't travel and shouldn't give money to help people overseas – but our travel should inspire us, and our giving shouldn't be an excuse to ignore the needs we can see among our own neighbours.

The genuine thing

In my home town I know a man who regularly takes meals to the old lady across the street who doesn't want to be put in a home and hates hospitals. He is certainly fulfilling the demands of true religion:

'Religion that God our Father accepts as pure and faultless is this: to look after orphans and widows in their distress and to keep oneself from being polluted by the world.' (James 1:27)

In fact, James has some pretty strong stuff to say about people who are poor and people who are rich. He reckons it's the rich who are badly off and the poor who are esteemed! Now, this shouldn't be an excuse for those of us who are rich to let people scrape by in soul-destroying poverty. It's not a loophole for the rich to be complacent and say, 'never mind, I've got money, but God values you more than me.' James is simply saying – watch your attitude. Don't look down on people who are poor, cos God certainly doesn't.

What if we had what they needed and we refused to give it?

Sometimes we're not going to know what to do for people we meet who are poor. Sometimes we will be ripped off and taken for granted. We may question whether what we are doing is really making any difference at all and begin to doubt that we can do anything to solve the problem of poverty.

But we shouldn't let our uncertainty or doubt paralyse us. It is better for us to err on the side of generosity, if we can, imitating God who is lavish and kind. In fact, God promises to reward us, in the mother of all parties, heaven itself, if we give to people now who can't repay us.

> 'Then Jesus said to his host, "When you give a luncheon or dinner, do not invite your friends, your brothers, sisters, relatives, or your rich neighbours; if you do, they may invite you back and so you will be repaid. But when you give a banquet, invite the poor, the crippled, the lame, the blind, and you will be blessed. Although they cannot repay you, you will be repaid at the resurrection of the righteous."' (Luke 14:12–14)

We should give without keeping accounts. We shouldn't be thinking, 'Whose turn is it?' In fact, God says it's much better for us if we hardly notice we're giving.

I know of someone who believed in church tithing (giving a tenth of their income to the church). A workmate, already seriously in debt, was struggling to pay their rent and threatened with eviction. So this Christian gave her tithe to the workmate and thought little more of it. She moved jobs and lost contact with her friend. Several years later, they met up. My friend had completely forgotten the gift. Her former colleague hadn't.

> 'So when you give to the needy, do not announce it with trumpets, as the hypocrites do in the synagogues and on the streets, to be honoured by men. I tell you the truth, they have received their reward in full. But when you give to the needy, do not let your left hand know what your right hand is doing, so that your giving may be in secret. Then your Father, who sees what is done in secret, will reward you.' (Matthew 6:2–4)

This doesn't mean that we should be naïve, because the Bible also says people should work for their food (2 Thessalonians 3:10), but it's about not being greedy and tight with the abundance God gives us.

And finally...

Whether we're rich or poor or somewhere in-between, God loves us and wants to do stuff with us. Just like working for justice, we can care for others out of the talents and money (or lack of it) that God has given us. To set up a soup kitchen or give someone a stack of money may be beyond us. To smile at the lonely person across the street isn't.

Chapter eleven

Life with enough

So what's the solution?

By now, we're probably not sure we want to pursue riches with the single-minded devotion that characterises loads of people in our society, but nor are we convinced we want to be living in some pit with boarded-up windows, rotten floorboards and fleas in the mattress, all because we say we love Jesus. Luckily, there is another way.

I think it's summed up in these simple verses from Proverbs 30, which is actually a prayer:

> 'Give me neither poverty nor riches,
> but give me only my daily bread.
> Otherwise I may have too much and disown you
> And say, 'Who is the Lord?'
> Or I may become poor and steal,
> And so dishonour the name of my God.'
> (Proverbs 30:8,9)

(In fact, Proverbs is a great book for sussing out stuff like wealth, poverty, work, wisdom and relationships.)

The writer here is getting at the idea of a moderate life, a life that God plays a part in, but not a life so poor that the person is scraping by, having to sin simply to survive. We don't want to be shoplifting to eat, nor do we want to be so diamond-drippingly rich that we forget God.

Pray the prayer

We can use these verses from Proverbs as our own prayer. It's bold, but good. We, too, can choose to live lives of moderation, lives without excessive wealth. We can avoid 'loadsamoney' and 'bling bling' and the contempt that comes with flaunting our riches. We can also avoid a life that has us rooting through other people's dustbins for our dinner. And we can be content and wisely generous.

The rewards of living with enough

I love this true story I heard of a computer programmer who developed a whole new way of computers running information. He didn't copyright it to himself in the hope he'd amass his riches by forcing people to buy his goods or by taking them to court if they abused a jealously-guarded copyright.

Instead, he put his first prototype up on the internet for other computer people to comment on, use, modify and change. By a process of collaboration and trust, he's now evolved a computer system that even the big-name companies buy into. And it's still all completely free. But it gets even better.

One company, in gratitude to this guy for letting them use his system, gave him a set of company shares. When the company floated on the stock market, the computer programmer became a multi-millionaire overnight. He sold the shares and now lives in a modest house with his wife and family and says he's a happy man.

Cynics will say, 'This guy could have had so much more.' But I'd rather point to this man and say, 'Here is a happy, contented and fulfilled person who has contributed to a better world.'

When full is empty

A cartoon I once saw showed a couple buying different products, going to the latest film and eating out in the coolest restaurant, but the last frame of the cartoon had the woman exclaiming, 'If I consume so much, why do I feel so empty?'

There is an emptiness that comes with chasing the latest must-have accessory to our life. That's not to say that we shouldn't have a table, chairs, a bed, lampshades, but do we need to replace them when they're not worn out? Do we need to store so much stuff we're unlikely to use again? Do we need fifty pairs of shoes, when it's unlikely we'll ever wear more than three pairs? If people can do life laundry just cos it's common sense, can't Christians do life laundry cos they know they're fulfilled by more than what they possess?

I watched a documentary about aid to Africa once. One woman had set up a shop selling second-hand clothes in her city. A couple of huge container-loads of clothes turned up every couple of weeks, from her overseas supplier. They were the stuff UK charity shops couldn't shift. As she opened one of these huge containers, out came clothes in all shapes and sizes, some brand new and never worn. But mostly red. Why red? Red just wasn't in that season, dahhling.

Free to be me

What of the perfectly good clothes we don't wear any more because they're just not the right colour? What of that mobile phone you bought two years ago, that still works, but which you wouldn't dare use for fear of being accused of owning a 'brick'? What about that T-shirt that doesn't have a label, let alone the right label? How can you turn up anywhere in it, including church?

You just do. You make a decision that says, these things don't matter. It doesn't matter if my clothes aren't the coolest cut – they fit me, I like them and I'm warm/dry, cool/comfy. So what if my phone isn't the one everyone else has? It works and it's affordable.

> You make a decision, and you pray for courage, and then you just begin to live the liberated lifestyle you're secretly drawn to, the liberated life that says 'I have enough and I am content'.

Believe me, your contentment will be far more powerful and challenging than the fact your shirt came from the second-hand shop and you're wearing the same sandals you wore last summer. You'll be free.

Free from the dictates of designers whose Caribbean holidays and worse, overseas sweatshops, are funded by your hard-earned cash. Free from the paranoia of 'not quite fitting in'. Free from shallow friends who only want to hang with you because they think your gear, but not you, is cool.

You'd be surprised who'll stick around though: the liberated and those longing-for-it. Some Christians, some non-Christians. Your stand against consumerism marks you out as a revolutionary, someone who is quietly changing the world, so that what you buy is no longer the measure of what you're worth.

Don't worry, though; it's not about donning a loincloth. It's simply about living with what you know you need, not with what others would like you to believe you need.

Does that mean I can never buy stuff again?

Does following God's view on money mean we never buy into anything literally again? No: it's not some hippy New World Order we're talking about here. Trade does exist and even people who are poor can benefit from trading.

When God set down a load of guidelines in the Old Testament for how a society should run, he didn't say, 'Now this money stuff, it's really not me, so let's scrap it.' God doesn't think we should avoid trade systems. Equally he's not so heavenly-minded he doesn't understand how the International Monetary Fund works (thank goodness someone does).

What God does say is, 'Let your money and your trading be totally rooted in justice.'

And in with that goes his characteristic concern about the poor.

The Old Testament tells farmers to leave stuff in the fields for the poor, not to clean up – it's called gleaning.

I heard on the radio that a high-street supermarket chain has decided to donate its £1 billion worth of used-by food (still safe) to the Salvation Army, rather than simply throwing it away. That's modern-day gleaning. In the Old Testament it was farmers. Today it's food multinationals. It's a different scale, maybe, but the same God-shaped ethic.

Great Aunt God

Equally, God doesn't say, 'Come away with me to a place free of interest rates, earnings and taxes; leave that dirty money and let's talk spiritual.' God's 'spiritual' is in the bank (or wants to be) as much as in the church, the hospital, the school.

God's not some fragile old aunt, who can't cope with the demands of the world or who'll be offended if we mention the 'm' word. We can make decisions about who to bank with, work for, get our money from, what we spend it on and how much and whom we give it to, and include God in the process.

More and more, people are asking for ethical funds, insurers, mortgage and bank deals. There is a demand out there and hopefully a lot of it is coming from Christians, people who want to live a moderate, simple, thoughtful lifestyle right here, right now, in reality.

Chill out

Life with enough leaves room for God and others. I think it's no accident that Jesus said the pagans 'run' after possessions – clothes, food, stuff. Have you noticed how tiring trying to keep up with things is?

I used to live near one of the biggest shopping centres in South-west London. Weekly, the equivalent population of Basingstoke would pass through my neighbourhood in search of the latest gear, from WAP phones to washing machines, sofas to sushi sets. Up and down the street they'd traipse, laden down by their many bags and purchases, kids bored or tired, bickering and drained by the new millennium hobby, shopping.

My friends and I didn't (and still don't) have that kind of money. So what did we do? We walked in (free!) beautiful places, we talked, we read, we slept, we chilled, we prayed, we laughed. And it was relaxing and enjoyable and made us all more fulfilled than stressing over objects that in a week's time would just fade into the background as yet something else we'd bought. Things that, in a month's time, we'd be cursing as so much clutter.

Running is tiring. Chasing riches is exhausting. But walking (and you'll notice we're advised to walk with our God) isn't. Out of breath? Maybe it's time to stop.

And if you're worried that not being fashionable, and not being stressed about stuff, is going to be a dull, monotone life, think again. Or rather, read this:

> 'Consider how the lilies grow. They do not labour or spin. Yet I tell you, not even Solomon in all his splendour, was dressed like one of these. If that is how God clothes the grass of the field, which is here today and tomorrow is thrown into the fire, how much more will he clothe you, O you of little faith! And do not set your heart on what you will eat or drink; do not worry about it. For the pagan world runs after all such things, and your Father knows that you need them. But seek his kingdom, and these things will be given to you as well.' (Luke 12:27–31)

Because you're worth it

You can do it. For every reason, including for yourself and everyone else, God wants you to be content and to live with enough. Enough so that there is space for him. Enough so there is space for all your friends and for the simple pleasures you really enjoy that have to do with the amazing person you have been created to be. Having a lot of money, having lots of possessions 'just because' is unlikely to contribute to your own or the planet's well-being. Life with enough, on the other hand, will.

Chapter twelve

Top tips for living life with enough

OK, you're convinced. You're up for it. Well, here's a practical starter. Try any or all of the suggestions below or mix 'em up to suit your own lifestyle and enjoy it. As you start to do some of these things more regularly, they'll become a habit and easier. (There's not even a mention of hair-shirts – trust me.)

Buying

- It is worth **considering your clothes**. Take a look. Are there any you haven't worn in the last year? Any that don't fit any more? Bag them up and take them to your local charity shop. (The same goes for CDs you don't listen to any more, books you don't read, stuff you don't want.) Enjoy your new uncluttered surroundings – and resist the urge to fill them up again.
- **Buy locally**. Support products you know haven't been flown thousands of miles, using fuel, to get to you. Think about farmers' markets (there're loads in cities, too) and local shops – or even pick your own in the summer!
- **Buy fairly-traded** if you can afford to – buy into a trade system that's fair and just.
- Don't be ashamed to **buy second-hand**. A friend of mine decided a second-hand cot would do for his first child (he checked it was fully safe). Whilst in the second-hand shop, he came across a rare video he'd wanted for years. It cost him 50p. Scan the local ads and try car boot sales, too.
- **Make a shopping list!** If you only need three apples in a week, only buy three. Don't be tempted by the big bag. Shop in a market, which is often cheaper (especially at the end of the day)

and has more local stuff. Eat foods that are in season, as they're also cheaper and more likely to be local.

- **Buy thoughtfully.** Will a more expensive but better-made brand of shoe in a classic style last you longer than the trendy purple platforms everyone's wearing? Probably. Have fun and be creative with what you wear, but be thoughtful about it, too.

- **Don't be taken in by the hype.** Do you really need shampoo with added Himalayan spring water and herbs harvested at midnight under a full moon? Or would a cheaper version do? No one's really going to know if you use the same shampoo as Jen 'n' Brad or not.

Sharing

- Spending **time with your mates**? Think of activities you can enjoy that don't involve visiting the cashpoint beforehand.

- **Live generously.** Model yourself on God. Got more dosh than you need, even after you've saved some? Take someone out for a meal. Buy a present for someone that you know they need but can't afford. Send extra dosh off to charity.

- A good time with mates is better than a five-course feast. If you **want to have a party**, but can't afford it, ask others to bring stuff. At a family get-together, invitees brought a savoury and dessert each and someone even contributed eight bottles of champagne they didn't want! Everyone felt more involved, less stressed and it was all about sharing time, food and company.

- **Skills share.** Do you have a skill others could use? Possessions you could share? Can you trade off the use of your PC against an arty friend's hand-made picture for your wall, for example?

- In Germany, several times a year, people pile their **no-longer-wanted items** onto the pavements and people are free to take away what they want. Could you develop this in your own neighbourhood or church?

Caring

- **If you're travelling**, don't bargain people down to the lowest level you can. Bargain them to a level you think is fair. I saw a trader in a Jerusalem market weep when a tourist haggled him down to a low price. Blockades on the city meant he hadn't been able to sell enough to buy his family food. It wasn't a ploy. The tourist could easily have afforded more.

- **Don't allow possessions to be a barrier to relationships.** Are people put off being your mate or coming to your church because you have too much? Would they be expected to pay for lots of things? Honestly look at your lifestyle and church and see where it could become simpler and more accessible to everyone.

Growing

- Do a Bible study on **God as your provider**. Recall times when you have known God has provided for you – perhaps money came to you as an unexpected gift when you needed it; maybe someone cooked you a meal. Is there space for God to give to you right now?

- Cultivate **trust in God**. Don't base your trust on your money or possessions. When you pray, tell him you trust him and mean it. Let the Holy Spirit challenge you about your lifestyle, remembering God loves you and wants the best for you.

- **Pray about stuff you need to buy.** It might sound over-holy, but plenty of people I know have ended up with cool boots/fab stereos/inspiring and beautiful clothes, all cos they invited God, the wildflower creator, into their retail therapy.

- **Be thankful.** Get into a habit of being appreciative of what you do have, for what's already around you. It's amazing how rich you'll begin to feel.

Living

If you want to think harder about wealth and your attitudes to it, **here's some questions to get you going**. You could work through them by yourself or with a group of mates. You don't have to do them all – just the ones that are relevant to you. And as always, you know you can chat about them with God, who isn't your bank manager, but someone who loves you and values you and is just waiting for you to say, 'Hey God, you know that wisdom thing...'

- What are you willing to do and not willing to do for money – eg would you compromise your morality for dosh?
- How much time do you want to have outside work – eg for hanging out, doing things you enjoy, meeting friends, getting involved in church?
- What can you do without? Make a list...
- What do you actually need and what are just things you are buying to keep up with everyone else? Remember, fashion is based on the idea that things quickly go in and out of fashion.
- When you do buy something, only have things that you know are functional and believe to be beautiful. Your turtle-print T-shirt may be hopelessly uncool, but it's comfy, fits you and makes you feel happy – and by 2022, everyone'll be wearing them... maybe.

SECTION THREE:

ECO-CHRISTIANITY

Chapter twelve

Going green

When I was 19, I nicked a book off my friend's shelf called *Going Green*. It was written by Jonathon Porritt, then the head of the Green Party and a big voice in environmental politics. He was a bit of an all-round cool geezer, having decided to live a rural existence while at university in a kind of hippy haven. I tried reading his book, but didn't get much past page 30. However *Going Green* stayed on my bookshelf and gave me a kind of thrill every time I spotted it. I thought it lent instant coolness to me and showed that I cared about both politics and the environment.

Why was it so cool to be into green issues? I guess because at that time Greenpeace seemed to be the only truly radical charity around. They were the ones sailing round whales in fragile-looking dinghies to protect them; they were the ones taking on the might of the multinationals and winning. They were the ones who really seemed to have conviction and have it large. In comparison, everyone else was still at school. These were the big boys and they had graduated.

Luckily, my commitment to environmentalism got beyond the doing-it-cos-it's-cool stage, perhaps surprisingly as I rediscovered God. It first started to happen during a typical student vacation. Every night, after finishing my work shift, I'd take myself off into the surrounding hills, lie down in a field and stare at the stars. I was going through a bit of a tough, soul-searching time, but there was something reassuring and comforting about lying on the warm ground and looking at the bright night sky. Looking back, I don't reckon it's stretching the truth to say I met Jesus in those fields.

Freaky? No. You know what? Such an experience is right there in the Bible.

'The Lord is my shepherd, I shall not be in want.
He makes me lie down in green pastures,
he leads me beside quiet waters,
he restores my soul.'
(Psalm 23:1–3)

That pretty much summed up my summer. But it's funny: even as I know that, I see the raised eyebrows. For Christians to care about creation, be affected by it or even have affection for it, is nothing short of dodgy when it comes to some 'Christian' points of view.

Creation myths

It seems to me that there are quite a few myths going round when it comes to Christians and the environment. Many either stop us from caring or give us excuses not to get our hands dirty in God's muddy old earth. First there's the...

New earth, new age

This is your standard, 'If it's anything to do with creation, it's New-Agey and dodgy and you'd better stay out of it.' But guess who created crystals? Er, yes, God. OK, maybe he didn't anticipate people writing whole books on how wearing them would enhance their lives, but they're a valid part of creation and appreciating their beauty isn't going to destroy our souls. If anything, it should help us understand a bit more about the beauty and wisdom of the Creator, the One described here:

'The Mighty One, God, the LORD, speaks and summons the earth from the rising of the sun to the place where it sets. From Zion, perfect in beauty, God shines forth.' (Psalm 50:1–3)

Staying out of creation, acting suspicious around it, is like a kind of watered-down version of Gnosticism, a brand of 'Christianity' which was doing the rounds during the early centuries of the first millennium.

Gnostiwhat?

Basically, Gnosticism said that anything material (whether it's your body or your back garden) is the opposite of anything spiritual. What's weird about this belief is that it seems to totally discount Jesus being human. Take a flick through any of the gospels and what do you find? A God who wafts around a few feet off the ground dispensing miracles while dressed in a floaty white number from Laura Ashley? Er, no.

> **What did Jesus do when he'd risen from the dead? Yep, ate a little fried fish with his mates. That's like you or me getting resurrected and going out for some fast food. Real? Bodily? You bet.**

Yes, there is stuff about new bodies (I'm hanging out for one that can find all its daily nutrients in a large tub of Ben & Jerry's ice cream), but that doesn't mean God despises what he made in the first place. Remember when he was on a roll back at the beginning of world history? He looked at people and said they were very good – and that was the naked version.

We need to get over this idea that God somehow hates the things he created. Yes, they/we're spoiled by sin and we live in a world that needs a bit of fixing. We suffer pain in our bodies and they don't work for all kinds of reasons, but does that mean they are duff? No, completely not. They are still amazing – and many brilliant scientists and doctors have already said so.

Body talk

What's more, we experience God in our bodies. We don't have some out-of-body experience.

We actually feel God's peace in our hearts and minds.
We feel his power, his touch, his comfort.
They are real and we really experience God.

We understand God by applying our brains and minds to him and the Bible. We see and smell and touch creation, including our family and friends, and we get an idea that God is awesome and worthy of worship. It's right there in the Bible:

'The heavens declare the glory of God; the skies proclaim
the work of his hands.
Day after day they pour forth speech; night after night they
display knowledge.
There is no speech or language where their voice is not heard.
Their voice goes out into all the earth, their words to the ends
of the world.' (Psalm 19:1–4)

The problem with New Age stuff is not that it goes too far, but that it doesn't go far enough. We should be saying to people who are into crystals and feng shui and meditation exactly what Paul said:

'For as I walked around and looked carefully at your objects of worship, I even found an altar with this inscription: TO AN UNKNOWN GOD. Now what you worship as something unknown I am going to proclaim to you.' (Acts 17:23)

Thomas Aquinas, a medieval Christian, said that other branches of thought, such as science, had stolen treasures that by rights belonged to Christianity. This is true of New Age stuff. Crystals, flowers, stones, rocks, an appreciation of nature, peace, a calm mind, a consideration for the body – these all rightfully belong to Christianity, to the God who is a creative genius and who loves us and shares friendship with us.

> **A God whose firstborn Son is a human being who ate fried fish and drank the very best wine and learnt from flowers and birds about the love of his heavenly Father.**

New Age? You wanna argue it with Jesus yourself?

Care about the environment? Got a PhD?

Next up as an excuse/barrier stopping us from getting into God's world is the idea that we have to be PhD-level scientists and conservationists to understand it and to make any meaningful difference. Yes, there are amazing scientists who are into creation – Einstein himself argued that you couldn't really get into the universe without starting to believe that there was the most wise, amazing designer behind it. These scientists, conservationists, marine biologists, foresters and climate changeologists make a big difference to the earth. But does this mean you have to get more than a C in your Science GCSE to appreciate God's world?

The way some books are written, you would think so. And it's true that some jobs in the world do call for people skilled and experienced in environmental stuff – if you are one of those skilled people who dreams of putting their talents to use for a healthier planet, you should do it. However, not having a clue about birds' migration patterns or an encyclopedic knowledge of insects isn't going to stop anyone from experiencing the total wonder that is in God's world.

Rolling up the earth

The third myth that stops us inheriting the earth is the idea that God doesn't care about it enough. I once watched an interview with a woman who went to a well-known church in London. She was giving the interviewer a glowing account of being a Christian, but it was becoming clearer and clearer that she wasn't particularly bothered what went on in the world. 'We're going to heaven and that's all that matters,' was the basic idea. When the interviewer pressed her about it, she simply put forward the idea that God was going to wrap up the earth at the end of time, so it didn't much matter what happened in the meantime. Perhaps her thinking was shaped by:

> 'Then I saw a new heaven and a new earth, for the first heaven and the first earth had passed away.' (Revelation 21:1)

Now, while I think heaven is going to be a blast, I'm not entirely convinced by this reasoning. First up, it seems to say that we as humans can exist anywhere and that that's OK. If you exist in a nice, secure, warm, five-bedroom detached house in North London, I guess that really is OK. But lots of people don't. Secondly, does this mean God wants us to live a really horrible life in a squalid, uncared-for, polluted earth, while we hang out for a better life in heaven? I really can't buy this.

> **God has created the world for our enjoyment now and as part of that enjoyment we need to look after it responsibly for each other.**

Showing now: Earth (U)

I once had the amazing experience of flying from Nairobi in Kenya (East Africa) to London (UK). The flight was ten hours long. I was sitting by the window and it was a cloudless day.

We took off from Nairobi in the early morning sunshine, over matchstick Masai tribesmen and their clumps of cattle, who cast long morning shadows over the dusty earth. Then we flew past Mount Kenya, visible from miles around, where the clouds actually traced the pattern of the wind in a circle around its summit. Next, we flew over Ethiopia, where dark red trails cut through green, tree-filled valleys and a large brown lake glinted in the morning sunshine.

Into Sudan, I could see amazing circles and oases in the yellow desert. Continuing over Egypt, huge cliffs of orange dunes rose up from the desert floor.

Next, the plane crossed over the coast of Africa and into the Mediterranean, where red tankers no bigger than a fingernail were cutting the white-flecked blue water.

Once over the sea, we flew on up between the Greek and Italian coasts, with their harbours of posh white yachts. After this came the Alps, whose snow-flanked mountains broke the drifting cloud and brought the ground alarmingly close.

In Austria, there were many tiny whitewashed towns with roads neatly radiating out from them, like spokes on a wheel. Further on, into Germany and the Netherlands we flew, over wide industrial rivers and tiny, well laid out fields of beige wheat and yellow flowers.

We briefly touched down in Amsterdam, where we needed to make a connection to the UK, the plane flirting with tiny beaches on the Dutch coast and casting a shadow in the clouds as we circled before landing.

Then it was up in a peak over the North Sea, before we began a descent into Heathrow. Over the mudflats of the Thames and its sluggish brown water, we followed the curve of the famous river to London's metropolis, row after row of houses and blocks, past Tower Bridge, the Oval cricketing ground (more like a rounded square) and the London Eye, which, even as we flew lower, was still no bigger than a 2p coin.

Lower and lower we flew over the grey and green city, past people playing tennis in the parks, and with the windows on houses and shops glinting brightly in the late evening sunshine. Finally I stepped off the plane with Nairobi's orange dust still bright on my trainers.

> **To have the world passing before your eyes like this was like watching the most amazing film. It was a gift – undeserved, unasked for, unexpected and absolutely awesome.**

Let's not allow myths to separate us from the gift of the world that God has already given. If you struggle with any of them, a top tip is to pray about it. Tell God that you respect the fact that he made and loves the world and ask him to open your eyes to its beauty, your mind to its wisdom and your heart to its wonder.

Then prepare to be blown away.

Chapter thirteen

Go wide, go deep

As well as removing the barriers to getting into environmentalism, we need to get a much wider understanding of what God is into. Then we might begin to understand why an issue like environmentalism shouldn't be restricted to a nice Harvest festival or even an alternative worship service, but should be central to our lifestyle as Christians. One way to do this for creation is to get into the idea of *shalom*.

Shalom – *God's wide word for peace*

Shalom is an amazing idea and I have to say a) I discovered it only recently and b) I am already a totally signed up, full-on fan of this ancient, biblical idea. But what is it?

Shalom is the word that's often translated in the Bible by our word 'peace'. Yet *shalom* is way bigger than a slightly OK feeling. At the heart of *shalom* is the idea of wholeness. Essentially it's to do with well-being – physical, mental and spiritual health. It's peace for the whole person and peace for the whole of creation.

Shalom is the opposite of destructive things like disease, breakdown and disorder. It's definitely not war, fear, despair or sin. God directs us into *shalom*:

He guides 'our feet into the path of peace'. (Luke 1:79)

God creates it and gives it to us:

'Peace I leave with you; my peace I give you.' (John 14:27)

Sweet dreams

Hopes and dreams of *shalom* can be seen in everything from movements for world peace, the United Nations and friendly alliances between countries to city-level cooperation between businesses and government for the benefit of the people, through Neighbourhood Watch schemes, residents' associations and into our own wishes for healthy, whole, sound relationships.

As Christians, even without knowing the word, we want *shalom* to break out. As humans, we dream it somewhere deep down, yearn for it and chances are, if you're reading this book, are prepared to be involved in bringing it about.

> **Yet your desire for peace is just the palest reflection of God's passion for it.**

God is so into the idea of wholeness, he even said the stones of the ancient temple in the Old Testament should be uncut (whole). He wasn't after some kind of kooky rustic look (I don't think...), but wanted a really physical reminder for the people of wholeness.

Day by day

As well as being The Big Idea, *shalom* is also rooted in the everyday and familiar, from whether we get enough sleep:

'I will lie down and sleep in peace, for you alone, O Lord, make me dwell in safety.' (Psalm 4:8)

to where we live :

'Build houses and settle down; plant gardens and eat what they produce ... also, seek the peace and prosperity (*shalom*) of the city ... pray to the Lord for it, because if it prospers, you too will prosper.' (Jeremiah 29:5–7)

Jesus and shalom

The main *shalom* person, of course, is Jesus. If Jesus and the angels have a constant saying, it's this: 'Peace to you, don't be afraid.' It's a welcome and a blessing that Jesus not only gives to his disciples, but wants to give to the whole world. Check him out weeping over Jerusalem. He said:

'If you, even you, had only known on this day what would bring you peace – but now it is hidden from your eyes.' (Luke 19:42)

The whole of creation is held together (that idea of unity and wholeness again) by Jesus and through him (Colossians 1:17).

Shalom, *it's real peace*

Not only that, but *shalom* actually emphasises the material – it's not just about fuzzy feelings or a feel-good worship session. The good news of *shalom* includes fullness of life and freedom from oppression and exploitation. Knowing this will make us want to leap into it for our lives – but how?

Well, we're told that justice and peace kiss each other:

'Love and faithfulness meet together; righteousness and peace kiss each other.' (Psalm 85:10)

> **One way, therefore, to find peace and experience**
> ***shalom* is to live and love a life of justice.**

On a personal level, it's like when you do or say something wrong. You know what you did or said wasn't right and it niggles away at you. When you put that situation right – apologise to your mate, say sorry to your mum, admit it wasn't the dog that ate your homework after all – you feel a whole lot better. The niggle goes away and you feel at peace again.

Right living, including justice, carries peace with it.

Another way to experience peace is simply to ask for it – 'Peace I give you; my peace I leave with you,' Jesus tells the scared disciples as he appears to them after his resurrection. We're his disciples too and chances are, he wants to bless us with *shalom* today. What's more, he promises us he'll give us anything (good) we ask for.

'You may ask me for anything in my name, and I will do it.' (John 14:14)

Being Mr Shalom, Jesus is more than likely to want to share a little around.

Shalom v rage

But can peace really happen in our world?

We're so used to seeing our world torn apart by conflict, blown up by terrorists, destroyed by humanity's own evil desires, and we get so used to feeling afraid, angry and insecure, it can be difficult for us to believe that there's another way to live on this earth that's chilled out and doesn't involve drugs.

> **Yet peace can and does happen in our own lives, right here, right now, right in the reality of them.**

I've seen this in my own life. Fresh out of college, I landed The Stressful Job (I wasn't unique in that…). Lots of people had already left this workplace because they were disillusioned or ill. Everyone around me was stressed – job prospects didn't look great and work pressures were increasing all the time. At least two people I knew had a 'breakdown'.

Added to that, I went to a church that seemed full of divisions and worry. So there was a period in my life when I felt surrounded by all those anti-*shalom* things like fear, worry, anxiety, job insecurity and illness. To say the least, it was exhausting.

Yet I still remember to this day the moment I lay down on my scuzzy bedroom carpet (I was too tired to sit, kneel, read my Bible or sing a worship song) and desperately prayed (not expecting very much of an answer), 'God, you must know the answer to stress. What is it?'

Now I'm not one of these people who have a mobile-phone level of attachment to hearing the Lord speak, but I felt sure the Lord whispered in my heart, 'Peace.' *Shalom*. And since I heard that simple word God has taken me deeper and deeper into peace. Not just spiritually, but physically, mentally and even emotionally. I'm not saying my life is a bed of roses and I wake up each morning with a perma-grin fixed to my face. But Jesus wants to take me and you and all of us deeper into him and his peace, as we go out to the world.

> **Peace is the total solution to all the stress we see, read about, hear and experience. We need to have a clear vision of *shalom* and a direct experience of it, so we can carry it with us into a hurting world.**

If you need *shalom*, just ask God to give it to you. It's that simple. Really.

Universal peace, like, yeah

So how does *shalom* relate to the environment and to creation? Luckily, *shalom* is such a friendly, inclusive idea that nothing is left out of its embrace, from what to do with the Millennium Dome (one suggestion was to convert it into a huge tropical-style garden area with green spaces and human-friendly accommodation – sounded like the architects for this had an instinct for *shalom*) to greening your local church. *Shalom* will take an issue and turn it around for people's and creation's benefit.

Getting a grip on *shalom* means the difference between thinking

God is somewhere out there in the hazy blue, his mind occupied by greater things than our dodgy accommodation or our rip-off landlord, to believing in a God who cares about real things in our lives, including even the smallest details like whether we sleep OK at night.

And it goes further than just us. *Shalom* wants to go out into the world and change stuff, and the world wants that to happen too. As the Bible says:

> 'The creation waits in eager expectation for the sons of God to be revealed. For the creation was subjected to frustration, not by its own choice, but by the will of the one who subjected it, in hope that creation itself will be liberated from its bondage to decay and brought into the glorious freedom of the children of God.' (Romans 8:19–21)

Notice that word 'decay'? Anti-*shalom*. It's a heart cry you probably feel yourself when you see people living in a derelict, urban wasteland where no one, least of all Christians, seems to care. But somehow, some of us, in some way or another, may be given the possibility and the privilege to bring *shalom* to pass in these environments, as fully paid-up, *shalom*-bearing, eco-Christians. If that's you, go there. Do it. Inspire.

Chapter fourteen

Eco-Christians in the city

It's all very well talking about *shalom* when we're thinking about God-made stuff like twinkly stars and rosy sunsets, but what about dirty, noisy cities? Is it possible to be an eco-Christian with a *shalom*-faith and live in a city. Possible? Sure is. Vital? You bet. Read on.

Sin city?

By the year 2030, over half the world's population are predicted to live in cities. In rich countries, the figure will be nearer eighty-five per cent. Chances are, as a student, you'll spend at least three years of your life in one. Cities already have a major impact on what happens to the environment.

Recycle, reuse, repair

Take London. Huge quantities of water, paper, plastic, wood and metal are used there every year. And how much of all those materials does it recycle? Three-quarters? A half? A tenth? No, lower than that. This huge city recycles just four per cent of what it uses. Where's the rest go? Put it this way, the earth is viewed by some people as just one big rubbish bag.

OK, some materials are burnt, but when we burn or bury our waste, poisonous substances can be given off, which affect air, soil, water and our health.

Sadly, wastefulness seems to be just part of the way London does things (in line with many other cities). Way back in the 1840s a chemist called Justus Liebig was urging the city authorities not to pump the city's sewage into the Thames. He wanted it treated and returned to the soil, so it could act as a fertiliser for growing crops. London had lots of crop growers within its boundaries, but the authorities turned a deaf ear and water pollution was born.

> **It's not just local problems that the city produces. Cities have the decision-making power to destroy entire ecosystems.**

How? Well, business can affect the environment and business decisions are largely carried out in big business institutions, like the London Stock Market and even parliament. It's no longer enough to target national logging companies in South America, for example – real power rests with corporations and companies and many of them have their headquarters in capital cities, like London.

Is it all bad news?

However, it isn't all doom and gloom. Research groups show how simple measures are effective. Green commuter routes (eg biking and bussing it to college or work) cut traffic. Safe routes to school mean single children don't have to be ferried around in the family's 4 x 4 or people carrier. Home deliveries by shops cut even more traffic. By doing just the three things above, experts reckon traffic could be cut by a third in just ten years. A third less traffic on city streets has to be a good idea. Less traffic means less noise, less pollution, less stress and better safety.

City suburbs, too, could produce a lot more of their own food, following the lead of Hong Kong, which has twice as many farmers per head of population as the whole United Kingdom – wouldn't it be cool to see farmers coming into city suburbs and taking over land to generate food, jobs and income? Even now, farmers' markets, where you can buy produce direct from the person who grew it, are becoming more and more popular and going deeper and deeper into the city. When I lived in a built-up city suburb, I had the choice of not one but three farmers' markets.

Do I have to knit my own yoghurts?

Public transport, recycling, and small markets trading local food are all things we, as Christian city-dwellers, can support and literally buy into.

We also can't duck out of environmentalism by saying it's a lifestyle for the rich. Yes, some stuff is really expensive (but do you really need a vest, let alone an organic, llama-hair one?) and personally I've never really had to face the issue of whether my coffee table is made from teak or mahogany, but we can do small stuff – sell on our second-hand books, recycle our magazines and newspapers, take our bottles to the bottle bank, put our old clothes in the clothes bank, wear a warmer jumper in winter rather than turning up the heating.

Being green doesn't necessarily mean knitting your own yoghurt or using home-made candles instead of bulbs (though there are some great energy-saving bulbs you can buy), but it does mean that, as a city-dweller and as a Christian, you can't not care.

If anything, what you do could have as much impact or more as anyone else living a neo-hippy lifestyle in the wilds of Wales (where, incidentally, public transport, buying local produce and recycling are still all possible and desirable).

Go deeper

Being an eco-Christian is about more than shopping. If all we are doing is swapping one set of shopping guidelines for another, however great our embarrassment at insisting we'll buy only human-rights-friendly trainers, it's just not going deep enough. We aren't touching the real reasons for going green as Christians.

> **It's not just about green consumerism – organic bananas over non-organic, hemp pyjamas over cotton, forest-friendly futons over beds direct from the logging companies.**

Nor are we going deep enough if we think being an eco-Christian is simply about what we do with our murky bath water. It's not just about biking to work instead of taking our car. Nor is it about whether your fleece has been made from recycled plastic bottles or whether you brushed your teeth with fluoride-free fennel toothpaste this morning.

> **Your green stars in God's eyes are not necessarily based on whether your back garden boasts a compost-munching wormery or plants that attract rare butterflies. And even though God may be applauding your bank account that only favours environmentally sound companies, to paraphrase Corinthians 13, if you ain't got love, it's nothing.**

This isn't to say make an eleventh commandment 'thou shalt care about the environment cos I made it'. The real shining truth for us green Christians is that we are aware of God's love and the totally high value God places on humans and how that relates to the environment around us.

> **Does God want people to live under noisy flight paths? It's doubtful. Stuck in a block of flats surrounded by a noisy ring road? Unlikely. Eating cancer-inviting, pesticide-soaked vegetables? Hmm, maybe not.**

Green and loving it

Christians can be and need to be at the forefront of the green revolution. Why? Because God values us and the world. It's as simple as that. And it needs to be a revolution with an 'access to all' sign high above it. It's Christians who should be coming up with plans to regenerate neglected and run-down city areas, Christians who should be lobbying in favour of environments that maximise the health and well-being of individuals, Christians who should be changing laws that currently favour large-scale, international, intensive farming over healthier, small-scale, local and organic farmers. It's just not good for us humans to live unhealthily, and God knows that and cares about that – and so should we.

Green houses

Let's take the hot issue of housing. In fact, housing is a major eco-issue whether you live in Buenos Aires or Bristol.

I remember walking round a slum in Delhi with a woman who was working as a town planner. She later wondered aloud to me what good her degree and her training was – shouldn't she be saving street children? I reminded her of some of the things we had seen in the slum – electricity being stolen illegally (and dangerously) by residents, poor sanitation, cramped conditions, four or five people sharing a one-room slum house, the fact that this slum could quite literally be washed away as soon as the rains came, as it was based in a dried-out river bed.

These are issues that town planners deal with directly. Why are floods so catastrophic in some parts of the world? Because they don't know they are coming? That's unlikely in somewhere like Bangladesh, which suffers from annual flooding. More likely, there is no one planning adequate housing to withstand flooding. Later I found out that, in another flood-prone part of the world, coastal inhabitants build houses on stilts that they can literally move up a hillside come tidal bad weather – now that's good planning.

The physical environment people live in is majorly important. Research in San Francisco has shown that the more traffic there is on a street, the fewer friends the residents have and the higher their chances of mental problems and heart disease.

In short, if you were responsible for creating a really excellent area of housing, not only would you have been responsible for roads, houses and traffic, but you might also have saved a child's life (from a fatal car accident), helped someone stay sane, cut the chances of another person having a fatal heart attack, safely housed the poor and destitute...

Our world needs Christians who are not only good scientists and conservationists (how many cures for life-threatening illnesses are being destroyed each day as another plant species is wiped out for good?), but also good planners, regulators, councillors – even people to be on the stock market shedding light and wisdom. All of these areas can be influenced by Jesus-loving people, who have whole, God-shaped ethics.

> As Christians, we can have a direct impact on some of the real environmental issues that affect people. The best thing is the way our care comes directly from the passion of God's heart and head to ours.

Chapter fifteen

Top tips for being an eco-Christian

Maybe caring about creation is a totally new idea to you. Maybe deep down you do, but you aren't sure how to express it. Wherever you are on the green scale, from caterpillar 'potential' to butterfly 'full-on eco-Christianity', here's some ideas to get you deeper into the world and into a creative, compassionate, wise and loving God. Go green, now.

Get wonder

- **Practise contemplation.** Really look at the world around you. Be open to awe and wonder, as you really look at a tree in blossom or the vivid colours of autumn.
- **Enjoy your God-given senses.** Go on a sense walk. For five minutes, concentrate on each of your senses – what you see, hear, smell, touch, even taste (eg wild blackberries or the air itself). Thank God for the reality and beauty of creation.

Open your heart

- **Pray for those who are sick**, remembering Jesus' firm intention to heal. Keep on praying for them, asking God to give you insight and wisdom on how to pray, remembering Jesus is concerned about a person's total well-being (*shalom*) – body, mind, spirit, heart.

Get inspired

- **Read stories** of people who have cared for the earth. How could their story inspire you?
- **Create**, and enjoy the process of creativity. You don't have to make a masterpiece – you can just enjoy the feeling of creating something: a poem, painting, story, song, photos, dance…

Read the Bible, knowing God cares about the earth

- **Try one of the Gospels** with an eye on the reality of Jesus' earthly life, from his stories about sparrows, to cooking fish on a beach, to the names of real places he visited.
- **Read Genesis 1 slowly**, the stuff that happened before the fall. Think about how God created and blessed everything, declaring it good.
- Choose some of your **favourite environmental verses** in the Bible and make pictures or posters of them (perhaps using natural ingredients).
- **Pick something you find in nature**, maybe your favourite thing – sun, sea, sky. Does the Bible mention it at all? Get a Bible dictionary and list every place in the Bible that mentions your fave thing, then look up each reference. Next up, think about what these verses tell you about God and the world.

Here's just some of the ideas that struck me by looking up passages about trees: God's relationship with people is rooted in the real, touchable, seeable world; God does stuff in real places at real times; judgement can come via creation; God is involved with creation and cares for it; creation is both beautiful and serves a purpose; humans are caught up in the creation song; prophets use creation to instruct and warn, via dreams, riddles and stories; Jesus uses nature to teach; heaven will have trees – material and real – and they'll help heal us.

Can you believe it? That's just your bog-standard humble old tree. (Don't worry if you don't get a whole long list of ideas – you only need one to inspire you.)

Enjoy the fresh air, green grass, birdsong...

- **Go on a walk** by yourself or with your local nature group (your local library will have details). Learn more about your locality, whether that's the bats who swoop at night or the one-legged cricket making its summer song (and that's just my local park).
- **Find a way of deliberately spending time outside** – playing sport, painting, drawing, photographing, sharing with friends (eg picnics), snowball fights (you know you want to...).
- **Invest in a bike** and cycle or walk whenever you can. Not only will you save money, but it's good for your body and your mind.

Expand your understanding

- **Learn about the indigenous groups of your land.** Read stuff about Celtic Christians who had a strong connection to creation and creativity.
- **Relate your spiritual journey to the seasons you experience.** If it's spring, think about what's blossoming in your life; if it's summer, can you find a God who loves to holiday?; what about autumn – what's bearing fruit in your life right now?; as for winter, it's not all doom and gloom – as you think about how the earth rests in winter, can you get into the idea of God nurturing and resting you?
- **Identify the plants and trees by name** that you can see out of your window. It's amazing how much this can root you in the real.
- **Educate yourself about wholesome, wholefood cooking.** Next time you eat or cook a healthy meal, really take time over it, savouring what you're eating. Rustle up a meal for mates and convert them to healthy eating, too. Remember: God in wisdom created food that is beautiful and healthy for us, too.

Nurture creation

- **Get into gardening.** No, really, why shouldn't you? Grow some of your own food or flowers where you live! You don't need a garden to do it. Borrow a book from your library on plants in containers or window boxes. Jesus learnt from nature around him. Let God use nature to speak to you.

- **Do something for the non-human elements around you** – put up a bird box or feeding table; nurture those straggly plants; plant a tree from seed; clean up litter; use eco-friendly washing products. Show you care practically.

Notice life around you

- **Notice the differences between the seasons**, even if you spend most of your day inside. Bring some of that new awareness into your daily environment – pebbles from the beach holiday, fir cones you collected on your woody walk, a winter scene on a postcard.

Organise change

- **Find out about recycling facilities** near you and make a conscious effort to use them. The more you do, the more of a habit (and the easier) it will become. Paper, wood, plastic, clothes, even Christmas trees can be recycled. Check the local paper or email your council (they'll have a website) for more details.

- **Take a mindful walk** round your neighbourhood, maybe with two or three others. Particularly think about how the neighbourhood benefits people (eg local park) and what it lacks (eg safe road crossing).

- **Pray and take action** on the things you see are lacking – perhaps a road crossing opposite the school or a heavily littered area near the old people's housing. Raise awareness of your concerns and get your neighbours involved too. Contact the council, if necessary, urging them to get involved.

- **Work together for a better environment for everyone.** If you live in halls of residence, are there recycling facilities? At church, do people use fairly traded coffee? Small changes add up to big differences.
- **Join a group lobbying for the environment**, for human well-being, for world peace. It could be small – your local halls of residence, the CU – or big. If you fancy a church-based one and there isn't one, consider setting one up. Use some of the ideas in this section to get you going as a group.

Well-being – get some

- Do things that **make your body feel good** – swim in an open-air pool, start to exercise with the intention of enjoying your body rather than punishing it for not being thin/big/muscley/strong/toned enough.
- **Enjoy your God-given health and vitality** – actually thank God when you are healthy, rather than just praying when you feel sick!
- **Pray for peace** in your own life and for God to spill it over wherever you are. Sorted.

Chapter sixteen

Conclusion

If this book's come over as just a list of rules and regulations you have to follow to squeeze yourself into the kingdom of God, if all you feel now is a truck-load of guilt and all you think is that your life doesn't measure up in God's eyes, then I've failed you.

Simple is about one thing – loving God, loving your life and trying, in the same imperfect way that every other Christian down the ages has ever tried, to love others. For some of us, that loving takes the form of caring about justice, peace and the environment. Our inspiration and ability to carry it off is always and only a personal relationship with Jesus.

If, on the other hand, you've seen and believed, perhaps for the first time, that God cares passionately about the universe and the people he's created, including you, then I've done OK. If you can see a way of taking that belief into your own life and influencing what's around you for good, then that's more than me. Maybe that's God nudging you, coaxing you and encouraging you to get involved.

Pre-heaven, we're always going to be working, struggling, sometimes succeeding, sometimes failing, often just persevering for the better world we know can exist and believe to be right.

> **We dream the dream that's on God's heart and then, with his help, in our own small way, try to make just a bit of that dream a bit more real.**

I hope you go on to do every good work that God imagined you doing when the stars of the universe were little more than a twinkle in the Great Creator's eye.

I hope that you find others to inspire you, encourage you and carry you and that you can do the same for them.

Wherever you are, remember a cloud of witnesses are totally for you and cheering you on. Whoever you are, wherever you live and whatever you get up to in your life: run your race. Act justly. Love mercy. Walk humbly.

You can. So do.

It's simple.

To purchase any of the following titles, or for further information on Scripture Union's full range of resources, visit www.scriptureunion.org.uk
or phone our Mail Order team on 01908 856006.

Dear Bob
Annie Porthouse

Jude Singleton is about to face the biggest challenge of her life...

... she is looking for a man.

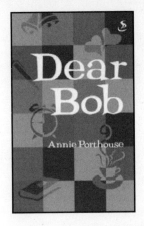

On the way to finding him, she
has to deal with those annoying
distractions of university life, broken
toes, waterproof curtains and driving
instructors with dubious breath.

Oh, and she is not sure whether there
is, or isn't, a God, the one foundation
she thought was there.

Dear Bob is the hilarious diary of Jude written to her future husband
whom she has named Bob, for ease of use. Join her as she spends
her first terms at University.

www.dearbob.com

£6.99
1 85999 633 7

A to Z of Being a Girl of God
Dawnie Reynolds-Deaville

Realise ur value
Realise ur potential
Rock ur world
This A–Z inspires you to be
A Girl of God

Dawnie Reynolds-Deaville brings the definitive A–Z of being a Girl of God in her own unique, in your face and street style. Starting with the Bible, each topic is saturated in soundbite, rhythm and rap, to inspire and empower. The book can be used individually, daily, to return to time and again, with others – or whatever way you want.

£3.99
1 85999 764 3

D-TOX

Interactive, online Bible reading from Scripture Union.

The ultimate D-TOX
D-TOX yourself
D-TOX your community
D-TOX your world

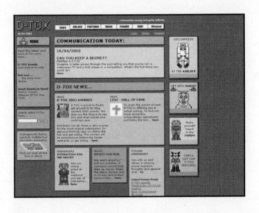

You can be transformed
Meet God through the Bible
Be changed
Change others
Change the world

www.d-tox.org.uk

Word up

Word up aims to help 11–14s grow in their relationship with God through reading the Bible together. Each book features two series of six 25 minute group Bible study outlines for leaders. Use them as part of a mid-week or Sunday session, or in your school Christian group.

£2.99 each

Word up: live it large
1 85999 647 7

Word up: the trouble with love
1 85999 612 4

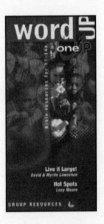

Word up: pressure points
1 85999 553 5

Word up: get real with God
1 85999 554 3